THE ADVENTURES OF DAVID FANNING IN THE AMERICAN REVOLUTIONARY WAR

ISBN: 978-0-919614-41-3

The Golden Dog Press gratefully acknowledges the
support accorded to its publishing porgramme by
the Ontario Arts Council and the Canada Council.

Ontario Arts Council
20th anniversary
1963-1983

Printed and bound in Canada.

THE ADVENTURES OF DAVID FANNING IN THE AMERICAN REVOLUTIONARY WAR

Edited by A.W. Savary

THE GOLDEN DOG PRESS, Ottawa, Canada

The Narrative of Col. Fanning

Introduction by A.W. SAVARY

COLONEL DAVID FANNING, of North Carolina, was one
of the most remarkable characters developed by the American
Revolution. His own narrative of his sufferings, exploits, marvellous adventures and hairbreadth escapes during the war has for
years past been an object of quest by writers and students of American and Colonial history, especially in the Maritime Provinces. It
was not until quite lately that I succeeded in tracing and getting
temporary possession of the manuscript, and to my surprise afterwards discovered that it had been printed—first at Richmond, Virginia, in 1861, "in the first year of the Independence of the
Confederate States of America," in an edition of fifty copies "for
private distribution only," with a preface signed "T.H.W." and an
introduction by John H. Wheeler, author of a History of North
Carolina, and that it was reprinted in New York in 1864 in an
edition of 200. The fact of these publications is not generally known
to American, and still less known to Canadian, readers of to-day.
Neither the first copy nor the reprint is entire or quite faithful to the
original, and both are out of print, and a complete and true copy
will, I am sure, be valued both in Canada and the United States.
Not only are the incidents related of thrilling interest, but the narrative is a self-vindication of one whom American writers of every
grade have agreed in execrating as the very incarnation of wicked-
ness and ferocity. It was not until about the middle of the last
century that the American public awoke to the fact that there could
have been any patriotism or public or private virtue in the breast of
any one who espoused the loyal side in the American Revolution. It
was the melancholy fate of a Loyalist to be written down a villain
before the eyes of posterity; and it has been laborious and difficult
to uncover and bring to light the real characters of many worthy

men from under the vast load of obloquy with which American writers had overwhelmed them. As an American *littérateur* of note once remarked to me, Sabine's "American Loyalists" was a "revelation" to the American people, who had never before known that there could possibly be two sides to the question. "Here then rests a Tory, and you say, judge, that he was a good man," exclaimed Sabine himself in surprise, when the grave of the Rev. Roger Viets was pointed out to him in Digby. Sabine, no doubt, was as impartial as he dared be in view of the public to which he was catering, and he ventured to record and condemn many of the violent excesses of the Whigs, but often fails to connect cause and effect in relating the reprisals on the part of outraged Loyalists which those excesses naturally provoked, and he enters no extenuating plea for Fanning, while as to Moody, whose similar narrative in full the reader will find in the "History of Annapolis," and who was pursued in his own State by the same vindictive hatred that followed Fanning in his, he diffidently concludes that "evidence is wanting to show that he violated to a serious extent the rules of civilised warfare." Both these men desired to remain at peace, but like many and many another similarly inclined were driven into the war by the homicidal or predatory violence of their rebel neighbours. As the numerous town histories of New England show, it was the function of the "Committee of Correspondence and Safety," organised as a sort of Inquisition in every township, to visit every man in the township and compel him to sign or refuse to sign a pledge to support the Continental cause with his life and property. Any who declined from conscientious religious scruples, as a Quaker, might be excused, and such was the number who sought immunity under this plea that the Reverend Jacob Bailey* wrote that he expected that at the close of the war, if the result should be favourable to the British cause, the Society of Friends would be found to have very largely increased. Those, however, who refused on any other ground were subjected to treatment in contrast to which the modern boycott were mercy itself. The cases of Moody, Budd,† Fanning and Thomas Brown, are only examples of an immense number whose story never has been and now never can be told. Tarring and feathering a neutral, or a "Tory," and carrying him astride a fence-rail, was a favourite pastime of "patriots" all over the country. Besides, pending the achievement of their independence, the various State governments assumed the prerogatives of recognised nations in respect to the *crimen laesae majestatis,* and

2

tried and executed as rebels against the State those who refused to be rebels against their king. Men who were unwilling to join in subverting by force the government *de jure,* were thus held guilty and made pay the fatal penalty of treason against the usurped government *de facto.* Two instances unrecorded in history come readily to my mind as I write: A brother of the father of the Honourable James W. Johnstone, the eminent Nova Scotian statesman and jurist, a mere boy, was so put to death in Georgia,* and one Hutchinson, son of the second wife of the Rev. John Wiswall, loyalist Rector of Aylesford and Wilmot, N.S., was hanged by the rebels when attempting to visit his parents.† These two cases are not mentioned by Sabine, and his book abounds in such. "Proscribed and banished" is the sentence he continually records, and the banishment was usually on pain of death.‡ Impartial historians cannot but put down these deeds as "cold-blooded murder," to use the exact term applied to Fanning's acts in the preface before me.

Nor does Sabine deal much more justly with the memory of Col. Edward Fanning and Richard Lippincott, known in this country after the Revolution as most worthy and estimable as well as able men, and as late as 1879, on the occasion of the bi-centennial celebration of Rochester, Mass., one of the orators of the day branded with shame the memory of General Timothy Ruggles, a native of the town, whose talents, and virtues would probably have made him President, perhaps the first President of the United States, as he had been of the first Congress of the disaffected colonies, if his conscience and judgment could have permitted him to espouse what proved to be the winning side. He fell, politically, in a lost, although an honourable and chivalrous, cause. But more recent American writers have been fairer than Sabine, and more courageous, and many of them are now treating the events of the American Revolution, and the characters and motives of its actors, in a judicial spirit. Doctor Hosmer, in his life of Governor Hutchinson, does full justice to his worthy and distinguished subject, but we are surprised that he justifies the expulsion of the Loyalists, not apprehending that the same spirit of chivalrous and religious fidelity that marked their dutiful allegiance to the old government would have been transferred to the new, once the terrible struggle in which they had fought and lost was over; and that the ability and patriotism of their leaders would have been of immense value in helping to overcome, instead of, as he suggests, promoting or accentuating the initial difficulties and troubles that unavoidably beset the new republic.

3

Sydney George Fisher, with obvious propriety, entitles his most valuable book, which has been very recently published, "A *true* History of the American Revolution." He faithfully exposes and accounts for the suppression and distortions of the truth by the earlier writers, but entirely misunderstands the modern colonial policy of England, and traduces her conduct of the Boer war. A perusal of his book is absolutely necessary to a fair understanding of the facts of the revolutionary period.

In Fanning's original manuscript the chirography is excellent, but there is little or no punctuation, and the orthography and too free use of initial capitals is perhaps a little more irregular than was common in those days, and these errors are aggravated and a distorted punctuation introduced in the printed edition. In fact, there is reason to suspect that the Richmond editor tried to make Fanning appear a more illiterate man than he really was.* It is better, I think, that all these eccentricities should be rectified in the present reprint, as manuscripts of that period are usually so dealt with in these days. It is satisfactory to note that Mr. Wheeler declares that the narrative "from its minuteness of detail and accuracy of dates (which have been compared with reliable authorities) may be depended on as a truthful record," and quotes the testimony of the historian Bancroft to its "authenticity, fidelity and value." But the author of the preface starts with an error as to Fanning's birthplace, which he says was in Johnston County, North Carolina, whereas Fanning declares in his will that he was the son of David Fanning, and was born at Beech Swamp, in Amelia County, Virginia, where his father left a considerable estate of which he was "the rightful heir," and which he still hoped at that date (1825) that his family might recover, although he had evidently given up, as irretrievably lost, his former possessions in North Carolina. The hope of recovering his Virginia property, it is clear, led him to refuse* to allow his narrative to be published, lest it should weaken his claim in that regard. Other statements of the writer of the preface respecting Fanning's boyhood and physical idiosyncrasies, given as "principally traditionary," such as his being afflicted with "scald head," and unfit to sit at table with his fellows or to sleep in a bed, and designed to stigmatise him as a degraded character, belonging to the dregs of society, are evidently unreliable, and of doubtful good faith. He speaks of the "self-satisfaction" with which, after relating his "cold-blooded murder of his neighbours and fellow-citizens," he applies to himself at the close of his "Address, to the Reader," the

4

words of the Psalmist: "Mark the perfect man and behold the upright, for the end of that man is peace." But this text is not in Fanning's handwriting, and was no doubt written there after his death by his widow or son. As to the alleged "cold-blooded murder" it will be seen that in every case Fanning specifically mentions the offence which the victim was condemned to expiate, always the cold-blooded murder by the victim himself, singly or with others, of one of Fanning's men or some other Loyalist. For instance, we find in his index: "Col. Lindley murdered and two men hanged for it." I will italicise this and several other instances in the narrative. I refer also to Fanning's account of the barbarous treatment by the insurgents of his companion, Thomas Brown, whose terrible reprisals on his persecutors are fully related by Sabine. Mr. Wheeler has not a word of condemnation for these atrocities; they do not shock him in the least; while the deeds of their avenger excite in him the most intense horror. He says in his copious and doubtless locally valuable biographical notes that Col. Balfour was "cruelly murdered" by Fanning, although he had read in the narrative that in a previous negotiation as to the terms of a proposed peace between the contending factions, Balfour had laid it down that there was "no resting place for a Tory's foot on the earth," showing that a cessation of hostilities could only be secured by Fanning's surrender and execution. The conflict, therefore, was renewed with more desperate and fatal fury, and seeing that certain death awaited him at Balfour's hands in the event of his capture, it is hardly to be wondered at that at their next encounter Fanning should try to get in the first shot, or should seek the first opportunity of slaying his intended slayer.

I conclude that Fanning has been grievously maligned by American writers, who have been unable to view his career with other than the jaundiced eyes of the partisan. If he had done just what he did in the American instead of the loyal cause, he would have been acclaimed as one of the bravest and best of their heroes. Mr. Wheeler says: "Had the daring, desperate temper of Fanning been elevated by education, chastened by religious influences, and directed in proper and patriotic channels, his name might have been associated with that of the Marions and Waynes of the eventful epoch in which he was notorious." To this I would say that if he had fought on the revolutionary instead of on the loyal side, Mr. Wheeler and every other American writer would have described him as a man whose "daring, desperate temper" was eminently "elevated by education," and "chastened by religious influences," as well as "directed in proper and patriotic channels," and truly illustrious among the Waynes and Marions of that eventful epoch. His enemies' reports of his character and conduct probably influenced the British government, by whom he was not treated with the same generosity as others who had done and suffered less. Mob violence and outrages on person and property began* with the insurgents; wrong begets wrong, and Fanning, resolute, daring and resourceful, fought his enemies with their own methods, the only methods available to him in a war that set family against family, and neighbour against neighbour, and was waged by small, irresponsible bands all through the Province, over which a reign of terror, appalling to contemplate, made wreck of the humane sentiments that cast a glamour over the operations of regular warfare between Christian nations. As each petty leader, fired with party rage or thirsting for revenge, gained a temporary advantage over his opponents,

Hope withering fled and mercy sighed farewell:

He was animated by a chivalrous loyalty to his lawful sovereign, and the idea of a "united Empire," at least as disinterested and quite as commendable as the similar sentiments which fired the breast of the most faithful soldier of the Union who fought in the great American Civil War, and he was patriotically devoted to the interests of his country as he saw them.

The author of the preface asserts that the people of the Southern States, "ere the actors in the old struggle had all passed away, were obliged to again draw the sword to protect their homes and firesides from an oppressor (the North), who attempted to impose on them burdens more odious than those they refused to bear from that nation to which they owed their existence as a people"; that the "mad efforts" of the North to subdue the South had "brought about the re-enacting of scenes such as disclosed by our veracious chronicler"; scenes, "at the recital of which decency revolts, and before the perpetrators of them even the Tories of the first revolutionary war might 'hide their diminished heads'." Americans of the present day will consider him as wrong in these extravagant pronouncements as we consider him in his estimate of Fanning.

Sabine, who, strange to say, knew nothing of this narrative, says that Fanning's correspondence (although where and how he got

6

access to it is hard to conjecture, and he could have seen but little of it) affords "ample evidence" that he was "often involved in quarrels with his neighbours," which is scarcely compatible with the fact that he was chosen three times to represent them in the Provincial Parliament, in which he sat as member for Queens County from 1791 to January 27th, 1801. His will, however, dated at Digby, March 10th, 1825, four days before his death, shows him to have had at that time some difference with Elkanah Morton, the Judge of Probate, a widely known and esteemed* but somewhat punctilious and stern magistrate and official, for he expresses a wish that he should have nothing to do with the probating of the will, but that some other judge should deal with it.

A sad and most extraordinary episode put an untimely end to his career in the legislature, by calling for the vacation of his seat, he being the only member of a British colonial legislature ever so affected. A black woman of bad repute, known as Sall London, charged him with an offence for which at that day there was no alternative but the death penalty. To the astonishment of the public he was convicted on her unsupported evidence, but the judgment was promptly nullified by the Governor of the Province, who was convinced that he had been falsely accused and wrongly convicted, and did all he could in such a case by exercising the "royal prerogative" in his favour. After this he* removed to Digby, Nova Scotia, near which he lived on a farm at the base of the picturesque mountain that lifts its lofty head between the town and the strait on the old road to Point Prim Lighthouse. Here still nestles cosily the old farmhouse in which he restfully passed the declining years of his chequered life, and here lived his son, Ross Currie Carr Fanning, when the writer knew him from the early sixties of the last century till his death.

In New Brunswick his name is perpetuated in a stream known as Fanning's Brook, forming part of the boundary line between Kings and Queens Counties on the west side of the River St. John. On this stream he built a mill, part of the dam of which still exists, and the cellar of his house can be seen about half a mile distant.† In his will, besides the mention of his inheritance in Georgia, he spoke of the claim his family had on the generosity of the British Government, but although that Government granted a pension to Moody's widow, nothing was ever done for the widow or children of Fanning.

7

In the cemetery of Holy Trinity Church, Digby, is a stone with the following inscription:

In memory of
Col. David Fanning,
who departed this life
March 14th, 1825,
in the
seventieth year of his age.

Humane, affable, gentle and kind;
A plain, honest, open, moral mind;
He lived to die, in God he put his trust,
To rise triumphant with the just.

On another stone near by, evidently erected by himself, is the following epitaph, curious for its "minuteness of detail": In memory of David William, son of David and Sarah Fanning, who died July 15, 1810, aged 16 years, II months, and I day, and II hours and 37 minutes.

He left a daughter, Ferebee, who married first Simeon Smalle, of Maine; second, Peter Hanselpiker of a New York Dutch Loyalist family, and left issue. His only surviving son, Ross C. C. Fanning, lived and died on the paternal homestead, where he conducted the farm and operated a carding mill. He it was who permitted Mr. Porter C. Bliss, on behalf of the Massachusetts Historical Society, to copy the manuscript, probably not long after his father's death. It is to be hoped he never saw the printed version with its "Introduction" and "Preface." He was a burly looking man with a somewhat austere aspect, and long a much respected and efficient Justice of the Peace. In the General Sessions of the Peace, which formerly regulated municipal affairs, he was recognised as a man of good judgment but of very determined will. He was born May 30, 1791, married Sarah Woodman of Digby, and died Sept. 8, 1871, leaving an estate of about $20,000 to be divided among five dauthters. Mr. Wheeler states that Rev. E. W. Carruthers, D.D., in a work entitled 'Incidents and Sketches of Character, Chiefly in the Old North State," 1854, has devoted more than 150 pages to the life and character of Fanning, and quotes Dr. Carruthers as saying that this son was a *Ruling Elder* in the Church. But he was a member of the Church of England until about ten years before he died, when he united himself to the Methodist Society, in neither of which Churches is there such an office as *Ruling Elder.**

8

I propose to omit the "Address to the Reader" and the instructions to the printer at the end, and to insert all that was omitted by Mr. Wheeler, including the adventurous escape to Florida and the West Indies, and the proclamation of amnesty or "Act of Pardon and Oblivion of the State of North Carolina," the latter to show how limited and illiberal was its scope.

----

*Manuscript letters of Rev. Jacob Bailey, Loyalist Rector of Annapolis. See "A Frontier Missionary." Boston: Ide & Dutton, 1853.
†History of Annapolis, p. 430.

*Recollections of a Georgia Loyalist, edited by Rev. A. W. H. Eaton, New York, 1901.
†MS. Letters of Rev. Jacob Bailey.
‡Three ladies of social distinction were attainted of high treason by the Legislature of New York, and banished on pain of death, the only instance where women were so treated in the history of the English people.

*For instance: The word *pursue* and all its derivatives are always spelled correctly in the manuscript, and always *persue* in the printed copy, but I have changed *was* to *were* in many places.

*A letter from him, dated in 1822, printed in Mr. Wheeler's introduction, points to this conclusion.

*It was not till after this paper was written that I found a complete confirmation of these conclusions in another fair and impartial American book recently published. Van Tyne, in his "Loyalists of the American Revolution," p. 184, says that the hanging of five Loyalist prisoners of war by the rebels, in North Carolina, led to reprisals which were continued in that region through the war, clearly referring to the events recorded by Fanning.

*See History of Annapolis, page 426.

*Not in 1790, as Wilson in his History of Digby says, nor in 1799, as stated by Sabine.
†For the facts mentioned in the preceding paragraph the writer is indebted to Dr. Hannay, the able historian and archaeologist of New Brunswick.

*The Rev. A. M. Hill, in a little book, "Chapters in the History of Digby," professes in a humorous vein to give the reason for this change of religion. Under the heading, "How Ross Currie became a Methodist," he says that Mr. Currie was "a perfect picture of a prosperous, contented farmer," but "not the gentlest of mortals or the meekest of men, for the law of heredity had made him obstinate, dogmatic and strong-willed." He was the owner of a pew in Trinity Church. It came to pass that the ladies "considered that more of the Earth's surface should be covered by them," and adopted hoop skirts. They got along with them tolerably well in the streets by "in extreme cases making detours, or describing a series of semi-circles" in meeting each other. The projection of some of the pews into the aisles, among them Mr. Currie's, "affected the graceful carriage of the fair dames," and threatened the crushing and destruction of the cherished garment. Appealed to to allow a part of his capacious and comfortable pew to be cut away, Mr. Currie indignantly refused, and when "some of the Wardens, probably henpecked husbands, armed with a saw, accomplished the work of demolition," Mr. Currie "renounced all connection with the Episcopal Church, consigned the thirty-nine articles to oblivion, forgot in his wrath Apostolic Succession, and became an ardent disciple of Wesley. Styles, fashions, hoops and skirts had carried the day in Trinity."

CHAPTER 2

COL. THOMAS FLETCHALL, of Fairforest, ordered the different Captains to call musters, and present two papers for the inhabitants to sign. One was to see who were friends to the King and Government, and the other was to see who would join the rebellion.

The first day of May, Capt. James Lindley, of Raebern's Creek, sent to me, as I was a Sergeant of the said company, to have his company warned to meet at his house 15th of said month. I did accordingly, and he presenting the two papers there were 118 men signed in favour of the King, also declared to defend the same, at the risk of lives and property, in July, 1775. There were several advertisements set up in every part of the said district, that there was a very good Presbyterian minister to call at the different places to preach and baptise children.

But at the time appointed, instead of meeting a minister we all went to meet two Jews by name of Silvedoor and Rapely, who, after making many speeches in favour of the rebellion, and using all their endeavours to delude the people away, at last presented revolution papers to see who would sign them; they were severely reprimanded by Henry O'Neal and many others. It came so high, that they had much ado to get off with their lives. The rebels then found that we were fully determined to oppose them. They began to embody in the last of said month; to compel all to join them, or to take away our arms. Our officers got word of their intentions. I then got orders from the Captain to warn the militia to assemble themselves at Hugh O'Neal's mill; which was done by several Captains' companies, and continued for several days under arms, and then both parties were determined on this condition, that neither party should intercept each other. This continued for some time, until the rebels

11

had taken Thomas Brown, who after that had the honour to be Colonel of the regiment of the East Florida Rangers, at Augusta, *burnt his feet, tarred and feathered him, and cut off his hair.* After he got so he was able to sit on horseback, he came to our post, and the rebels then began to embody again. Col. Fletchall found a large camp, and marched from Liberty Springs to Mill Creek on our way towards Ninety-Six. Twelve miles from Ninety-Six the rebels found that they were not strong enough for us, and sent an express to Col. Fletchall to come and treat with them, which said Fletchall did. But the terms of their treatment I don't know. We were all dismissed until further orders. In a short time after, the rebels took Capt. Robert Cunningham and carried him off to Charlestown. Our party was then informed of his being taken off in the night time, and by making inquiry after him, we got information of a large quantity of ammunition that was there, on its way to the Cherochee Nation, for Capt. Richard Paris to bring the Indians down into the settlement, where the friends of the Government lived, to murder all they could. We intercepted the ammunition and took Capt. R. Paris, who swore to these facts. We then formed a large camp, and Col. Fletchall, being so heavy, he gave up the command to Major Joseph Robinson.

In the month of November, 1775, the South Carolina Militia, of which I was at that time Sergeant, under the command of Major Joseph Robinson, laid siege to a fort, erected by the rebels at Ninety-Six, commanded by Col. Mason; which continued for the space of three days and three nights—at the expiration of which time the rebels were forced to surrender, and give up the fort and artillery. Major Robinson then ordered the militia to the north side of Saluda River, and discharged them for eighteen days. Afterwards orders were issued for all Captains to collect their respective companies at Hendrick's Mill, about twenty miles from Ninety-Six; the rebels having received intelligence of our intended motion, they immediately marched before us and took possession of the ground, which prevented our assembling there. But about 300 of our men met at Little River and marched thence to Reedy River, and encamped at the Big Cane Break for several days. The rebels being informed of our situation, marched unexpectedly upon us, and made prisoners of 130 of our men; the remainder fled into the woods and continued there with the Cherochee Indians until the 18th January, 1776, when I was made a prisoner by a party of rebels commanded by a Capt. John Burns, who after detaining me four days and repeatedly urging me to take the oath of allegiance to the United States, stripped me of everything, and made me give security for my future good behaviour, by which means I got clear. On the 10th of May, 1776, hearing the rebels had issued a proclamation to all the friends of Government, offering them pardon and protection provided they would return to their respective habitations and remain neutral, induced me to return to my home, where I arrived on the 15th of June.

On the 20th, the rebels being apprehensive of the Cherochee Indians breaking out, dispatched several of their emissaries among the Loyalists to discover their intentions, one of which was Capt. Ritchie, who came to me and told me he was a friend to Government, and some time before left the Indian Nation, and then wanted a pilot to conduct him to the Indian Nation again. I agreed to conduct him to any part of the country he wanted to go to, provided he would keep it secret. This he promised to do. But immediately he went and lodged information against me, and swore that I then had a company of men ready, in order to join the Indians. In consequence of this, I was made prisoner again, on the 25th, by a Capt. John Rogers, and thrown into close confinement with three sentinels over me. On the 1st of July, the Indians came down into the back country of South Carolina and killed several families, at which time, the rebel camp being in great confusion, I made my escape, and went to my own house at Raebern's Creek; but finding a number of my friends had already gone to the Indians, and more disposed so for to do, I got twenty-five men to join me, and on our arrival at Parisher's plantation, on Reedy River, in the Indian land, we formed a junction with the Indians. On the 15th inst., in the evening, the militia and the Cherochees to amount of 260 surrounded the fort built with logs, containing 450 of the rebels, and after a smart fire on both sides for two hours and a half, we retreated without any injury except one of the Indian Chiefs being shot through the hand. I then left the Indians and pursued my way to North Carolina, where, on my arrival, I was taken up again and close confined, but was rescued by my friends three different times, after which I made my escape good. I then endeavoured to go home again, and after experiencing numberless hardships in the woods, I arrived the 10th of March, 1777, at Raebern's Creek, South Carolina.

I was made prisoner again on the 11th, by a Capt. Smith, bound hand and foot, and carried under guard towards Ninety-Six gaol;

after marching twelve miles, the company halted for the evening, and watching an opportunity I cut the ropes I was bound with and stripped myself when the guard was asleep; I threw myself out of the window and returned back to Raebern's Creek by a different way from that which they had carried me prisoner. I was obliged now to secrete myself in the woods, and was supplied with provisions by some Quakers and other Loyalists in the neighbourhood.

A company of Loyalists, of which I was one, was then raised by a Richard Parish, and it was determined to go to Mobile and join the British army, but one of the company proving treacherous, gave information to the rebels, who raised a body of troops to suppress us. They took me, with five more prisoners, and carried us to Ninety-Six gaol on the 5th August, 1777. Captain Parish escaped with some Loyalists belonging to the company, and made his way good to the British army at Mobile, in West Florida. Myself, with five others who were taken, remained in close confinement until November following, and we were tried for our lives on a charge of high treason for rising in arms against the United States of America, but were acquitted and went home. The fees and expenses of my confinement amounted to £300, Virginia money, allowing dollars at six shillings each, which I paid, and was then ordered back to the gaol for the rent of the room.

On the 1st of March, 1778, Capt. John York, of East Florida, received orders from the Commander-in-Chief for the Loyal Militia of Georgia and South Carolina to assemble themselves. Accordingly, they were embodied. The majority of the people chose me their commanding officer. We took a number of prisoners, furnished ourselves with horses, and marched to Savannah River on the borders of Georgia (two miles above Augusta). Capt. York, who was our pilot, then got discouraged, and would not suffer any of the militia to proceed with him back to East Florida except three men; we were then under the necessity of returning home, upwards of one hundred miles, through the rebel country, and betake ourselves to the woods as formerly. During our retreat we were pursued by three hundred of the rebels, but we got back home to Raebern's Creek safe. When the rebels found we were returned, they raised a body of men to take us, and for the space of three months kept so constant a look-out that we were obliged to stay in the woods; six weeks of which time I never saw a man, except Samuel Brown (who was afterwards killed at Tigo River), who shared my sufferings, and we lived entirely without either bread or salt, upon what we killed in

14

the wilderness. We determined, let the consequences be what they would, to proceed to the settlement of Green River, North Carolina, where we rested ourselves at a friend's house about a week. Here we parted. I then proceeded to Tigo River, where I arrived safe on the 1st of June, 1778. Myself and one Samuel Smith now associated and were taken by a company of rebels, commanded by a Capt. Going. We made our escape the second night by bribing the sentinel, and parted company. I met with one of the horses belonging to the rebels, about a mile from the house I had escaped from, and mounted him. They pursued me through the woods by the horse's tracks upwards of seventy miles, and came to Raebern's Creek where I lived. They were anxious to recover their horse from me, and promised to return one of four they had taken from me if I would deliver up the said horse. This being agreed upon, I went with them to receive my own horse back again; when we had advanced thirty miles we came near to where a rebel fort was. I desired them to go a little out of the way and avoid it, which they had promised to do before we proceeded on our journey. One of them laid hold of my horse's bridle and told me to surrender myself a prisoner, for they were determined to confine me in the fort or carry me to Ninety-Six gaol, about eighty miles off. They said I was not in that damned tory country at that time. I therefore, after some conversation, concluded to submit to be disarmed at the time, as they threatened blowing a ball through me every instant if I did not surrender, which I did. On my arrival at the fort I was stripped of my clothes and confined close till morning, when they tied my legs under a horse's belly and took me before a magistrate to commit me to gaol. However, I was admitted to bail for my good behaviour. On my return to the people who took my horse and clothes, upon asking for them I was retaken before another magistrate, and committed to gaol under a strong guard. On my proceeding towards the gaol the guard was particularly careful about securing me; and in order to do it the more effectually, tied me with a rope to a stout fellow who was one of them. When I found him asleep I took the opportunity to cut myself loose with a knife (or rather with a pair of horse fleames) which was accidentally left lying in the road, and throwing myself out of the window made my escape, and took to the mountains for shelter. I continued there for some time, when Col. Mills of the Loyal Militia, on knowing where I was, proposed at several meetings we had, to raise a company, which we did, of 500 men, for the purpose of going to St. Augustine. One of the

15

company proved faithless and gave information to the rebels, who immediately embodied themselves and took Col. Mills prisoner with sixteen of the company, and carried them off to Salisbury gaol. Myself, with fourteen more, pursued about twenty miles with an intention of rescuing them, until we were in sight of Gilbert town where the rebels had a guard; and finding we could not effect our purpose at that time, our numbers being so small and theirs increasing, we returned back. The rebels pursued us all night, and in the morning we perceived them within shot of us. We fired upon them, which they returned, and continued skirmishing with them in the woods about an hour, when they retreated. What injury we did them we could not tell; on our part we suffered no loss. Here our party separated, and I made way for Holsten River, about 140 miles through the woods. I had proceeded about forty miles on my way when I was met by three men, one of whom knew me. He came to me with seeming friendship, and on taking my hand called his companions to assist him in securing me, which they did, and made me a prisoner. They tied my hands behind my back, and feet to each other under the horse's belly, and took me to Ninety-Six gaol again, where I was closely confined for seventeen days. During my confinement I got acquainted with a friend to Government, who lived there, by talking to him through the gates; he furnished me with two files and a knife, by which means I cut through the iron bars and escaped. I returned again to Raebern's Creek, and after remaining some time in the woods there I was advised by friends to make peace with Capt. Gillian, who commanded a company of rebels on the Indian lines. As I durst not be seen by any of the rebel party, I got one of my friends to go to him, desiring him to meet me alone at a particular place, and give him my word I would not injure him. We met accordingly, and passed our words not to disturb or injure each other. We continued our meetings in the woods, generally every day or two for the space of a month, until we were discovered by some of his company, who threatened to have him punished for treating with me. However, he still met me, now and then, and introduced a friend of his to me, who, he told me, I might depend upon. One day I observed an alteration in their behaviour, and asked them, when at some distance, if he meant to keep his word with me; he replied, "by all means." We were all on horseback, and I had my rifle across my saddle. When we were going to part, as I expected, he suddenly seized my rifle, and the man who was with him laid hold of my horse's bridle. He presented his rifle to my breast and told me I was his prisoner or a dead man. I was under the necessity of surrender, and they carried me again to my old quarters at Ninety-Six, where we arrived on the 11th of October, 1778. I was stripped entirely naked, thrown into irons and chained to the floor, and remained in that situation until the 20th of December following, when I again made shift to get my irons off, and having sawed one of the grates some time before, I again escaped by means of a fellow-prisoner, who supplied me with some old clothes, of which I made a rope to let me down. I received a fall in getting down, but luckily did not hurt myself. The gaoler heard me fall and presented a musket at me out of a window, but I avoided him. He alarmed the guard and they pursued me; but, however, I got clear off. I found myself much hurt by a fall I got in their chasing me. I got back to Raebern's Creek, but was taken in three days, and again introduced at Ninety-Six. I was chained and ironed as before, in the centre of a room thirty feet square, forty-five from the ground, the snow beating in through the roof, with four grates open night and day. I remained in this state eleven days. I got my chains off in the night of the twelfth. The gaoler did not chain me down again, but I had still part of them remaining on one of my legs, which weighed seven pounds and three-quarters. I continued loose in gaol until the 13th of February, 1779, when I took a bar out of the window in the night, and pried one of the planks out of the floor of the room and thence went down stairs. I found the door fast secured, but I went to a breach I had formerly made in the back of the chimney, and got out, and one of my fellow-prisoners escaped with me, and we kept together for some time after. We found a number of horses grazing in a field belonging to a company of rebels, under the command of Capt. Farr, who had that night come into town. We mounted each of us one and rode off to Raebern's Creek. On our way, we stopped at a house, and furnished ourselves with a rifle and a pair of pistols; we also supplied ourselves with clothing. By this time the neighbourhood was alarmed, and the rebel militia sent in pursuit of us. They laid several ambuscades, but without effect, and continued embodied for six months. But, however, I was so fortunate as to escape; but my companion was taken. The day after he was taken I was riding through a piece of timbered woods, when I discovered a party of men—they discovered me, and pursued on full speed for seven miles, but I was lucky enough to escape them, but my horse falling, threw me, and I unfortunately lost my rifle. An advertisement was then made public for apprehending me, and a reward of seventy silver dollars and 300 paper ones was offered as a reward to take me. This made me very cautious, notwithstanding which I was betrayed and fired upon by a party of rebels, in number sixteen; I received two bullets in my back, one of which is not extracted. I luckily kept my seat in the saddle and rode off. After proceeding about twelve miles I turned my horse into the woods, and remained there eight days, having no support but herbs, except three eggs, my wounds at this time being very troublesome and offensive for the want of dressing. I got my horse again and moved about twelve miles to a friend's house, where on my arrival I made a signal, which they knew, to acquaint them of my being alive, and a young girl of fourteen years old came to me; but when she came near enough to see me she was frightened so at the sight she ran off. I pursued after her on horseback, telling her who I was. She said she knew it was me, but I was dead; that I was then a spirit. I was a long time before I could get her to come to me, I looked so much like a rack of nothing but skin and bones, and my wounds had never been dressed and my clothes all bloody. My misery and situation was beyond explanation, and no friend in the world that I could depend upon. However, these people seeing me in that distressed situation, took the greatest care of me, and dressed my wounds. I then got assistance and support, and my wounds dressed and taken good care of. My horse having been seen by some of the rebel party, they concluded I was not killed, and wrote several letters, which they gave one of my friends, offering to treat with me, and advising me to surrender, threatening at the same time, in case I did not, to banish eight families of my friends out of South Carolina. A limited time was given for my answer, but it had expired before I received the letters; in consequence of which their threats were put in execution, and the people's properties were taken from them, and themselves confined. On the receipt of my letters the people were liberated, but their properties were still detained.

The second day after, I treated with the Colonel of the rebel militia, and had an express sent off to Gov. Rutledge at Charlestown. About a week after his answer came back with a conditional pardon, that which I had done should be forgotten, and that I should live quietly and peaceably at home, and be obliged to pilot parties through the woods as occasion might require.

Before I accepted of these conditions I advised with my friends and company, who all approved of it, as it conduced both to their ease and safety.

18

I remained at home a year and twelve days, and was repeatedly urged to accept of a company in the Continental service, which I always refused.

After the reduction of Charlestown, one William Cunningham and I concluded to embody a party of men, which we effected.

We determined to take Col. Williams of the rebel militia prisoner, and then to join Capt. Parish, who was to raise a company and assist us. Col. Williams got notice of it and pushed off, and though we got sight of him he escaped us.

We now found ourselves growing strong, and numbers flocking daily to us. I then took the King's proclamations and distributed them through the country for upwards of a hundred miles.

Capt. Parish had the command of the party and marched up to Ninety-Six, which he took possession of without firing a shot; where I found him again. The day after, we marched about twelve miles to Gen. Williamson's at Whitehall, who commanded a fort with fourteen swivels and two companies of provincial troops. On our approach he met us about three miles from the fort, attended by several officers, requesting that he might discharge the troops and have protection for himself and them.

We granted him what he requested, and took possession of the fort and their arms which they piled up; after that they marched out of the garrison.

Three days after that, Col. Pickins, with 300 men, marched in and laid down their arms.

General Robert Cunningham of the Loyal Militia now took the command, and formed a camp.

We kept scouting parties through the country and had many skirmishes, but none of consequence.

After the British-American troops had taken possession of Ninety-Six, I continued scouting on the Indian lines until Col. Innis forwarded his march up to Musgrove's Mill, on the Innoree River. I then joined them with a party of fourteen men.

The morning following the pickets were attacked by a party of rebels. Col. Innis ordered us to advance and support them, which we did, and followed them until we arrived where the main body lay in ambush, under the command of Col. Williams. Col. Innis was unfortunately wounded, with several other officers.

We engaged them for some time, and then retreated about a mile and a quarter, where we encamped, and in the night marched off towards Ninety-Six, under the command of Capt. De Peyster, and the next morning I and my small party returned back to the Indian lines. We continued scouting on the lines for some time, until I met with Capt. Parish of the British-American South Carolina Regiment, who gave me a list of several soldiers that had permission to visit their friends in the country. On the return from Florida to Ninety-Six, I was desired by him to go to give them notice to join their regiments; and on this expedition I fell in with Major Furgesson's party, which was defeated five days afterwards. The rebels after that began to be numerous and troublesome; and little or no regulation amongst us, I made the best of my way to Deep River, North Carolina, where I remained until the month of February, 1781.

I was, during this time, discovering the disposition of the people. Being informed that Lord Cornwallis was marching that way, I kept my intentions secret until I received certain accounts. I then caused this advertisement to be published, and used all my influence to get all the Loyalists to join me and defend ourselves when occasion might require. A true copy is here set forth:

ADVERTISEMENT

Any of his Majesty's loyal and faithful subjects, able and willing to serve in the Royal North Carolina Regiment commanded by Col. Hamilton, are hereby requested to repair to his encampment. The Bounty allowed for each man is three Guineas; and the terms of the engagement are that he shall serve during the rebellion and within the Provinces of North and South Carolina and Virginia only; that during his service he shall be entitled to clothing, pay, provisions, and all the advantages of his Majesty's Regular and Provincial Troops, and at the end of the rebellion, when he becomes discharged, of course, he is to receive as a reward for his services during the war a free grant of land agreeable to his Majesty's proclamation.

Of his pursuing Gen. Greene as far as Hillsboro, this struck such a terror on the rebels and was so pleasing to us, that we immediately disarmed the disaffected, and embodied about 300 men under the command of Col. Pyles. He fell in with a party of rebels (Col. Lee's dragoons), and lost twenty men killed, besides the wounded that died afterwards. At this time I was with a small party at Deep River, where I took two rebel officers prisoners and several soldiers. I then directed my march to the place where I left Col. Pyles and came within a little distance of the dragoons that had cut him up, when I was informed of his misfortune by some of his party that had fled; we then separated into small parties and took to the woods for some time.

The day Lord Cornwallis defeated Gen. Greene at Guildford, I was surprised by a Captain Duck, with a company of rebels, where I sustained the loss of all our horses, and arms; we had one man killed on each side.

The day following, myself and three more of the company furnished ourselves with arms, and pursued the rebels, who we discovered had parted and gone to their respective homes with their plunder. We visited one of the houses and found fourteen horses which had been taken from the friends of the Government; and discovering one of the said party in an outhouse, I fired at him and wounded him in the neck with buckshot, but he escaped. We then mounted ourselves and turning the other horses into the woods we returned back to Deep River. We kept concealed in the woods and collected twenty-five men, having scouts out continually until we proceeded to Dixon's Mills, Cane Creek, where Lord Cornwallis was then encamped. On our arrival there his Lordship met us, and asked me several questions respecting the situation of the country and disposition of the people. I gave him all the information in my power, and leaving the company with his Lordship, I returned back to Deep River in order to conduct more men to the protection of the British arms.

Two days following I returned to the army at Chatham Court House, after being surprised and dispersed by the rebel dragoons, on my bringing in seventy Loyalists. I joined my company again and went with his Lordship to Cross Creek, and as we had lost most of our horses, we determined to return to Deep River and join his Lordship when on his way to Hillsboro. General Greene followed his Lordship as far as Little River, and then returned to Ramsey's Mills on his way to Camden; his men marched in small parties and distressed the friends to Government through the Deep River settlement. I took eighteen of them at different times, and paroled them, and after that we were not distressed by them for some little time. After a little while some of us had assembled at a friend's house, where we were surrounded by a party of eleven rebels under the command of Capt. John Hinds. We perceived their approach and prepared to receive them. When they had got quite near us, we ran out of the doors of the house, fired upon them, and killed one of them; on which we took three of their horses and some firelocks. We then took to the woods and unfortunately had two of our little company taken, *one of which the rebels shot in cold blood, and the other they hanged on the spot where we had killed the man a few days*

21

before. We were so exasperated at this that we determined to have satisfaction, and in a few days I collected seventeen men, well armed, and formed an ambuscade on Deep River at Coxe's Mills, and sent out spies. In the course of two hours one of my spies gave me information of a party of rebels plundering his house, which was about three miles off. I instantly marched to the place and discovered them in a field near the house. I attacked them immediately, and kept up a smart fire for half an hour, during which time we killed their Captain and one private on the spot, wounded three of them, and took two prisoners besides eight of their horses, well appointed, and several swords. This happened on the 11th May, 1781. The same day, we pursued another party of rebels and came up with them the morning following; we attacked them smartly and killed four of them on the spot, wounded three dangerously and took one prisoner with all their horses and appointments. In about an hour after that, we took two men of the same party, and killed one more of them. The same evening we had intelligence of another party of rebels, which were assembling about thirty miles off in order to attack us. As I thought it best to surprise them where they were collecting, I marched all night and about ten o'clock next morning we came up with them. We commenced a fire upon each other which continued for about ten minutes, when they retreated. We killed two of them, wounded seven, and took eighteen horses well appointed. We then returned to Deep River again. I still kept the company together and waited for another opportunity, during which time I took two rebel soldiers and paroled them, who gave me information of a Col. Dudley coming from Gen. Greene's camp at Camden, with baggage.

I mounted my men and set forward in search of them. I concealed my men by the side of the road; and I thought the time long according to information I had from the soldiers. I took one man with me, and went to see if I could make any discovery. I rode a mile and a half when I saw Col. Dudley with his baggage. I then wheeled my horse and returned to my men. When I came within a hundred yards of them, Dudley and his dragoons were nose and tail, and snapped their pistols several times. I then ordered a march after them, and after marching two and a half miles I discovered them, and immediately took three prisoners, with all the baggage and nine horses. The baggage I divided among my men, which according to Col. Dudley's report was valued at £1,000 sterling. I returned to Coxe's Mill and remained there till the 8th June, when the rebels embodied 160 men to attack me, under the command of Cols. Collyer and Balfour. I determined to get the advantage of attacking them, which I did with forty-nine men in the night, after marching ten miles to their encampment. They took one of my guides, which gave them notice of my approach; I proceeded to within thirty steps of them; but being unacquainted with the ground advanced very cautiously. The sentinel, however, discovered my party, and firing upon us retreated in, where they secured themselves under cover of the houses, and fences. The firing then began, and continued on both sides for the space of four hours, being very cloudy and dark, during which time I had one man killed and six wounded, and the guide, before mentioned, taken prisoner, *whom they killed next morning in cold blood.* What injury they suffered I could not learn; as the morning appeared we retreated, and returned again to Deep River, leaving our wounded men at a friend's house, privately.

The rebels then kept a constant scouting, and their number was so great that we had to lie still for some time; and when Collier and Balfour left the settlement, the said Col. Dudley, before mentioned, took the place with 300 men from Virginia. He took a negro man from me and sold him at public auction among themselves for £110; the said negro was sent over the mountains, and I never saw him since. At length they all began to scatter, and we to embody. William Elwood being jealous of my taking too much command of the men, in my absence, one day persuaded them that I was going to make them regular soldiers, and cause them to be attached to Col. John Hamilton's Regiment, and vindicated it by an advertisement that I had handed to several of the Loyalists that I thought had the greatest influence with the Loyalists. He so prevailed with the common sort, that when I came to camp I found most of my men gone; I then declared I never would go on another scout until there was a field officer. The majority chose me; they then drew up a petition to the commanding officer of the King's troops.

A general meeting of the Loyalists was now called, in order to appoint a commanding officer of the militia; it was still determined that I should be the person. I accordingly set off for Wilmington, 160 miles, with a petition of the people to the officer commanding at that post for his approbation. On my arrival there, Major Craigg, who was commander, treated me with every respect in his power, and approved of said petition and gave me a commission as Colonel of the Randolph and Chatham Militia—a copy of which is hereunto annexed:

23

By James Henry Craigg, Esqr.; Major in his Majesty's 82d Reg., command-
    ing a detachment of the King's Troops in North Carolina, &c., &c.
To David Fanning, Esqr.

These are to appoint you to be Colonel of the Loyal Militia in Randolph
and Chatham Counties, who are directed to obey you, as such, in all lawful
commands whatsoever, and you are authorised to grant commissions to the
necessary persons of known attachment to his Majesty's person and
Government, to act as Captains and subalterns to the different companies of
militia aforesaid. As Colonel, you are hereby fully empowered to assemble
the militia, and lead them against any parties of rebels or others the King's
enemies, as often as necessary—to compel all persons whatsoever to join
you, to seize and disarm, and when necessary to detain in confinement all
rebels or others, acting against his Majesty's Gov't; and to do all other acts
becoming a King's officer and good subject.

Given at Wilmington, this 5th July, 1781.

J. H. CRAIGG,
Major Commanding the King's Troops.

On the 12th July I returned from Wilmington and ordered a
general muster, and then gave the following commission to the
gentlemen hereinafter named, of their respective companies:

By David Fanning, Esq.
Colonel of the Loyal Militia of No. Ca.

To _____ Greeting

Having received sufficient testimony of your loyalty and zeal for his Majesty's service, and relying on your courage and good conduct, I do hereby
appoint you to be _____ of a company in the district of _____.
You are, therefore, diligently and carefully to discharge the duty of such;
obeying all orders and directions which you may receive from time to time
from any superior officers in his Majesty's service, and all others; the inferior
officers of his Majesty's subjects of that and every other company are directed
and requested to obey you as _____ of said company.

Given under my hand at Coxe's Mill this ____ 1781.

DAVID FANNING
Col. Com'g his Majest's Loyal Militia, &c.

CHAPTER 3

ON my return to Deep River I immediately caused a general muster of the loyalists, which I collected to the amount of 150 men, but finding them deficient in arms I discharged all of them except fifty-three, which I appointed fully; out of which I collected from the whole, and ordered the rest to be ready to join me when I called for them. I also gave the foregoing commissions to the different officers set forth, who rendered many services to the British Government during the late war, who signalised themselves with me in the interior parts of that rebellious country, and subdued the greatest part of the province; so far that the worst of rebels came to me, begging protection for themselves and property. The exertions of myself and the other officers had the whole country under the protection of the British Government until long after the surrender of Lord Cornwallis and the evacuation of Wilmington; and after all the British troops were called to their different posts on the seashore I continued acting in the interior parts of North Carolina, and was like to obtain a truce with the rebels in the heart of the country. Those people have been induced to brave every danger and difficulty during the late war rather than render any service to the rebels, had their properties real and personal taken to support their enemies, the fatherless and widows stripped, and every manner of support taken from them, their houses and lands and all personal property taken, and no resting place could be found for them. As to placing them in their former possessions, it is impossible—stripped of their property, driven from their homes, deprived of their wives and children, robbed of a free and mild government, betrayed and deserted by their friends, what can repay them for the misery? Dragging out a wretched life of obscurity and want, Heaven, only, which smooths the rugged paths, can reconcile them to misfortune.

Numbers of them left their wives and children in North Carolina, not being able to send for them owing to the distresses, and now in the West Indies and other parts of the world for refuge, and not returned to their families yet. Some of them, that returned under the Act of oblivion passed in 1783, were taken to Hillsboro and hanged for their past services that they rendered the Government whilst under my command. I am fully sensible of the good designs that government intends for the loyalists in so repeatedly renewing the Act. If the inability and distressed situation of those people, who have suffered and experienced everything but death to support British Government, cannot reap the fruits of their labours, and now join under every species of mortification, I can solemnly declare that I think Major John Rains and Capt. George Rains two of the most deserving officers that ever acted in America during the late war, either in the provincial or militia; and to my certain knowledge John Rains had two mills burnt, three dwelling houses, and besides a barn and property totally taken away. I have given as direct account of the officers opposite their names as I possibly can; also their promotions and deaths. What I have set forth, I will forever vindicate. Besides other officers of other counties that joined me at different times and places, as I shall refer to in other parts of my journal, in particular Col. Arch. McDougald and Samuel Andrews, who joined me several times.

Given at King's County, New Brunswick, Nov. 29th, 1789.

The rebels on the same day held a general muster at Chatham Court House, about twenty-five miles from where I had assembled, and the day following were to call a Court Martial for the trial of several loyalists who had refused to bear arms in opposition to Government. Upon receiving this intelligence I proceeded towards the Court House, 17 miles, that night, with the men I had armed, and the morning following, by seven o'clock, I arrived there. I surrounded the place, where I expected to find members of the Court Martial, but they had dispersed the evening before, and were to meet at 8 o'clock. I then posted pickets on every road, and within the space of two hours took fifty-three prisoners—among them the Colonel, Major, and all the militia officers of the county, except two, who had not attended, and also one Continental Captain, with three of the delegates of their General Assembly. I immediately marched them to Coxe's Mill, and paroled all except fourteen, who I knew were violent against the Government. Those I conducted to Wilmington and delivered to Major Craig. I then represented to

26

Major Craig that with his approbation I would establish certain regulations for the conduct of the militia, which he approved of; and he was obliging enough, on my giving them to him, to correct and confirm the following rules, which were printed and distributed in the country:

RULES and REGULATIONS for the well governing of the Loyal Militia of the Province of North Carolina:

1st. No person to be admitted a militia man until he takes the oath of allegiance of his Majesty, which is always to be done before the senior officer of the Regiment on the spot.

2nd. All persons once enrolled in a militia company, and having taken the oath above mentioned, will be considered as entitled to every privilege and protection of a British subject, and will, on being detected joining the rebels, be treated as a deserter and traitor.

3rd. Every militia man is to repair, without fail or excuse, except sickness, at the time appointed, to the place assigned by his Colonel or Captain with his arms and accoutrements, and is not to quit his company on any pretence whatever, without the knowledge and permission of his Captain or Commanding Officer.

4th. The Colonel of every county has full power to call his Regiment together, and march them when necessary for his Majesty's service; the Captain of each company has also power to assemble his company when any sudden emergency renders it necessary, and which he is to report as soon as possible to his Colonel.

5th. Mutual assistance is to be given on all occasions, but as it is impossible to give positive directions on this subject, it is left to the discretion of the Colonels of Regiments, who must be answerable that their reasons for not affording assistance when required, are sufficient.

6th. When the militia of different counties are embodied, the senior officer is to command; Colonels of Regiments are immediately to determine the present rank of their Captains, in which regard is to be had to seniority of commission or service. In cases of vacancies the Colonels may grant temporary commissions, till recourse can be had to the Commanding Officer of the King's troops.

7th. The men are to understand, that in what relates to the service they are bound to obey all officers, though not immediately belonging to their own companies.

8th. Courts Martial may sit by the appointment of the Colonel or Commanding Officer; and must consist for the trial of an officer, of all the officers of the Regiment he belongs to, except the Colonel or Commanding Officer; and for the trial of a non-commissioned Officer or Private, of two Captains, two Subalterns and three Privates—the latter to belong to the same company as the person to be tried; the eldest Captain to preside; and the sentence of the Court to be determined by plurality of votes, and approved by the Commanding Officer.

9th. No Colonel is to supersede an officer without trial; but he may suspend him till he can be tried.

10th. Quitting camp without permission, disobedience of orders, neglect of duty, plundering, and all irregularities and disorder to be punished at the discretion of a Court Martial constituted as above mentioned; and by the approbation of the Colonel or Commanding Officer, who has power to pardon or remit any part of a punishment, but not to increase or alter it.

11th. Every man must take the greatest care of his arms and ammunition; and have them always ready for service.

12th. When the militia is not embodied they are at all times to be attentive to the motions of the rebels; and immediately to acquaint the nearest officer of anything he may discover, who is to communicate it to his Colonel or other officers, as may be requisite.

13th. It is the duty of every person professing allegiance to his Majesty to communicate to the Commanding Officer of the nearest British port any intelligence he can procure of the assembling or moving of any bodies of rebels. Persons employed on this occasion shall always be paid.

14th. Colonels of Regiments may assemble any number of their men they think necessary, to be posted in particular spots of their districts—their time of service on these occasions is to be limited; and they are at the expiration of it to be relieved by others. Great care is to be taken that no partiality is shown, but that each take an equal proportion of duty; for which purpose alphabetical rolls are to be kept, by which the men are to be warned. Every Captain is to keep an account of the number of days each man of his company serves.

The strick observance of the above regulations is strongly recommended as the best means of giving to the King's faithful subjects a manifest superiority over the rebel militia; and to insure them that

28

success their zeal and spirit in the cause of their country entitle them to expect.

Head Quarters, Wilmington, 25th Sept., 1781.

I then thought prudent to administer the following oath of allegiance unto those people I was dubious of: "I—A B—do swear on the Holy Evangelists of Almighty God to bear true allegiance to our Sovereign Lord, King George the Third, and to uphold the same. I do voluntarily promise to serve as militia, under any of the officers appointed over me; and that I will when lawfully warned by our said officers, assemble at any place by them directed in case of danger, in the space of eight hours. I will go, with my arms and accoutrements in good order, to suppress any rebels or others, the King's enemies; that I will not at any time do, or cause to be done, anything prejudicial to his Majesty's Government; or suffer any intercourse or correspondence with the enemies thereof; that I will make known any plot or plots, any wise inimical to his Majesty's forces or loyal subjects, by me discovered, to his Majesty's officers contiguous, and it shall not exceed six hours before the same is discovered, if health and distance permit. This I do solemnly swear and promise to defend in all cases whatsoever. So help me, God!"

I then returned to the head of Little River, on my way to Coxe's Mill, where I was met by two men who informed me that the rebels had separated into two small parties, thinking I should never return from Wilmington. I passed on and got intelligence of Col. Alstine lying on the banks of Deep River with a party of twenty-five men. We marched all that day and night following, and just as the day dawned we advanced in three divisions up to a house they had thrown themselves into. On our approach we fired upon the house, *as I was determined to make examples of them, for behaving in the manner they had done to one of my pilots, by name Kenneth Black.* They returned our fire, and the action continued upwards of three hours, when after killing four of them and wounding all the rest, except three, they sent out a flag to surrender, Col. Alstine's lady begging their lives; and on her solicitation I concluded to grant her request. After the capitulation I gave the following paroles to Col. Philip Alstine and his men:

"I do hereby acknowledge myself a prisoner of war upon my parole to His Excellency Sir Henry Clinton, and that I am hereby engaged till I shall be exchanged, or otherwise released therefrom, to proceed immediately to my plantation on Dunham's Creek,

Cumberland County (or elsewhere) in North Carolina, there to remain, or within five miles thereof—and that I shall not in the meantime do, or cause anything to be done, prejudicial to the success of his Majesty's arms; nor have intercourse or hold correspondence with the enemies of his Majesty, and that upon a summons from his Excellency, or other persons having authority thereto, I will surrender myself up to him or them, at such time and place as shall hereafter be required.

PHILIP ALSTINE,
Colonel.

Cumberland County,

Deep River, July 29th, 1781.

Witness: DAVID FANNING, *Colonel Commanding Loyal Militia.*"

In the course of this affair we had two men killed and four wounded, who afterwards recovered. A party of rebels appeared in sight a little time after the firing began, but they did not approach to afford Col. Alstine any support. When the action was over they ran off, and our horses being quite fatigued, rendered it impossible for me to pursue them, and I then pursued my route to Coxe's Mill, where, on my arrival, I gave twelve hours' leave to the men (after detaining a sufficient number for the necessary guard) to go to their respective homes. Immediately after that I heard that a waggon loaded with salt for the use of the rebel army had passed about twelve hours before. I took eight men with me, and after a chase of sixteen miles I overtook it and conducted it back to Coxe's Mill. On my return I found that Major Rains had been attacked by a party of 150 rebels, who had attempted to secure the fort of Deep River, at Coxe's Mill; however, it was without success. He had one man wounded and several horses in the attack, and on my approach they retreated. They then sent a flag with offers of peace. I returned for answer, "I was determined to make peace with the sword—or otherwise they should become subjects of Great Britain." My men now being collected to the amount of 140, who by this time were well armed, and hearing nothing further from them the next morning, we marched to the place where I had been informed they were, but found them gone off. I discovered some of their scouts, but on firing on them they took to the woods. I heard that they had marched and joined another party of 250 men, commanded by Cols. Paisley and Balfour, upon which I returned to Coxe's Mill; I sent out spies that night, who returned before morning and informed me that the two rebel parties had joined, being about 400 in number, and encamped at Brown's plantation, about two miles up the river on the opposite side. I dispatched a flag to them, acquainting them, as before, of my determination in support of Government, and proposed a meeting of both parties to determine the matter by force of arms; *at the same time acquainting them that the ill-treatment of some prisoners they had taken a little time before had determined me to retaliate in case an end was not put to it, should any in future have cause to complain.* I directed the flag to Major Cage, who commanded at the time before, and I received the following answer:

"SIR,—I received yours by a flag, and can assure you that I should be as sorry as any person living to misuse a prisoner; but at the same time I think it is my duty to oppose my enemies, and if any of your men should fall into my hands I shall endeavour to use what influence I can to have them treated as prisoners; and I hope you will do the same. I must also inform you that I am not the commanding officer; if I was, I should immediately return you an answer, and as your letter was not directed to the commanding officer, he will not undertake it without you will direct to him. Col. O'Neal is Commander at present.

I am, Yours, &c., &c.,

WM. CAGE.

Aug. 2nd, 1781.

To Col. David Fanning."

I also received a message from Col. O'Neal that wherever they met me they would fight me, but not by an immediate appointment. I directly ordered a march and proceeded to the place where I was informed by the bearer of the flag they lay encamped; but on my arrival there, they had marched off. From intelligence I had procured, I had reason to suppose they had gone to Salisbury to be reinforced by General Rutherford. I then concluded to go to Wilmington for a supply of ammunition, finding my stock began to grow low. I got to Cross Creek on the 11th of August; and early in the morning following crossed Cape Fear River, when Maj. Samuel Andrews joined me with his company and scouted through all the rebel settlements on the north side of the river, and took a number of prisoners, arms and horses. I also discovered where twenty-five barrels of salt was concealed, designed for the rebel army. I destroyed it, and then marched down the side of the river and came to a plantation belonging to a Capt. Robertson, which I burned. Thence I marched to his brother's, Col. Robertson, which I served

31

in the same manner. On my march I took several prisoners, whom I paroled, except twenty; those I delivered to Capt. Legett, then commanding at Wilmington, where I arrived on the 24th. Having got supplied with ammunition, I proceeded up the country on the 26th on my march to Elizabethtown, where on my arrival I found Col. Slingsbee, of the Loyal Militia of Bladen County, with a number of paroled rebels in his camp. I disapproved of keeping them there, and told him I thought it imprudent and unsafe. The event proved so; for that night they having arms concealed, fired upon his camp and wounded him mortally. Five captains also were wounded, some of whom died afterwards of their wounds. The day following I arrived at McFall's Mills, about sixty miles, where I despatched ninety of my men back to render assistance, on receiving the unfortunate account of Col. Slingsbee's misfortune; but it was too late, as the rebels had taken to the woods and got off.

I here had information that the rebel Col. Wade with 450 militia was then on his march to attack Col. McNeal, who had assembled seventy of the Loyal Militia of Bladen, and then lay on the side of Drowning Creek. I instantly despatched an express to know his situation, and offering assistance; in three hours I received for answer he would be glad to see me and my party. I marched direct, and by daylight arrived there with 155 men. Our pickets were fired upon, and retreated into camp, having exchanged several shots with those of the rebels. We had information they were crossing a bridge on Drowning Creek, about three miles off, when the pickets fired on them, and retreated to the camp, who informed me that 420 men crossed that bridge. I immediately ordered all my men to arms, and counted them; which in number was 225, horse and foot. I then marched immediately to attack them. When I formed my little party I left great vacancies in order to appear as numerous as possible, and to prevent their turning my flanks. We attacked them at 11 o'clock, and engaged them an hour and a half, when on my ordering a charge, they retreated. We pursued them seven miles, and took fifty-four prisoners, four of whom died that night. On our return we found nineteen dead, and the next day several came in and surrendered, all of whom were wounded, and we had reason to suppose that several died in the swamps, by accounts we received from those who came in afterwards. Our loss was only five men wounded, one of whom died, and five horses killed, besides a few wounded. We took 250 horses, most of which were loaded with effects they had plundered from the friends of Government; and as I had formerly ordered that whoever found concealed goods of any kind should hold them, I also now ordered that every man should keep that he had taken that day, after mounting and equipping those fifty who were not mounted in the action. I then paroled the prisoners, except thirty of them, whom I sent to Wilmington under a guard of Col. McNeal's men. Then, with my party, I marched that evening to Little River, sixteen miles from McFall's Mill, where the party returned who had gone to Col. Slingsbee's assistance. The day following I arrived at Coxe's Mill, thirty miles, where I issued the following advertisement, and circulated it through the country:

"ADVERTISEMENT

"This is to let all persons know that do not make ready and repair immediately to camp, that their property shall be seized and caused to be sold at public sale; and if they are taken and brought into camp, they shall be sent to Wilmington as prisoners, and there remain as such in the provost and be considered as rebels; also, if any rebel is willing to surrender and come in he shall reap the benefit of a subject.

DAVID FANNING,
*Col. Com'g Loyal
Militia.*"

*Camp Coxe's Mill
6th Sept., 1781*

On the 9th of Sept. I was joined by Col. McDougald of the Loyal Militia of Cumberland County, with 200 men; and Col. Hector McNeal,* with his party from Bladen of seventy men; and in consequence of my advertisement I had also 435, who came in; and many joined me afterwards.

I had previously determined within myself to take the rebel Governor Burke of North Carolina, and I had a conversation with Maj. Craig on the subject. I now thought it a favourable opportunity, as I found myself at the head of 950 men of my own Regiment, exclusive of McDougald and McNeal's regiments. I acquainted Maj. Rains of my resolution, who approved of it. The rebel General John Butler, and Col. Robert Maybin, of the Continental line, lay within forty miles of our encampment on the Cape Fear River, with 400 Continental soldiers and Butler's militia. It was supposed by my officers that I intended to attack them. After marching sixteen miles to Rocky River, I went a little distance out of my road to a friend's house, for intelligence of the situation of the rebels; during which time the guide led my little army about two miles out of the way, towards General Butler. On my return above to them I was under the above necessity of making my intentions known; and immediately directed my march for Hillsboro. I pushed on all that day and the following night; at seven o'clock on the morning of the 12th we entered the town in three divisions, and received several shots from different houses. However, we lost none and suffered no damage, except one man wounded. We killed fifteen of the rebels, wounded twenty, and took upwards of two hundred prisoners; amongst whom were the Governor, his Council, and part of the Continental Colonels, several captains and subalterns, and seventy-one Continental soldiers out of a church. We proceeded to the gaol and released thirty loyalists and British soldiers, *one of which was to have been hanged that day.* About 12 o'clock I left Hillsboro, and proceeded eighteen miles that night towards Coxe's mill; in the morning I pursued my march about eight miles further, to Lindsey's Mill on Cane Creek, where General Butler and a party of rebels had concealed themselves. Col. McNeal, who had the advanced guard, had neglected to take the necessary precautions for our safety; and by information of Capt. McLean, Cumberland County, Little River, as soon as I had discovered the situation we were in, and having so great a number of prisoners, I left my station and pushed for the advanced guard; on my coming up with Col. McNeal, I inquired the reason of his neglect, and before he could answer we were fired upon by the rebels. They killed eight men, among whom was Col. McNeal, who received three balls through him, and five through his horse. I then ordered a retreat back to where I left the prisoners, and after securing them, I made the necessary preparations to attack the enemy, which we did; and after engaging them four hours, they retreated. I lost twenty-seven men killed, and sixty so badly wounded that they could not be moved, besides thirty slightly, but so that they could keep up with our main body. At the conclusion of this action I received a shot in my left arm, which broke the bone in several pieces, and the loss of blood was so great that I was taken off my horse and led to a secret place in the woods. I then sent Lieut. Woleston to my little army for Col. Arch. McDougald and Major John Rains and Lieut.-Col. Arch. McKay to take command; to send an express to Wilmington for assistance, as I was not able to take any command. I also desired that Major Rains should return as soon as he could leave Col. McDougald, as I thought he might be the means of saving me from the hand of my enemies. These gentlemen conducted themselves in such a manner that I think they deserve the applause of every loyal subject both for their valour and good conduct, as Col. Maybin and General Butler pursued them all the way until they met Major Craig coming to their assistance. They made their march good for 160 miles, and never lost one prisoner, but introduced Thos. Burk, their Governor, and his regiment of rebels to Major Craig, who very well accepted them; and Major Craig introduced his Excellency and regiment to the Provost Master. I am informed by letters from Col. Arch. McDougald, dated 6th Aug., 1789, that no provision has been made for him yet. Also Major Rains the 2nd of October, 1789. But I am in hopes when the Government comes to be informed of the many services that they have done, they will consider them, and make some allowance for them. I am personally acquainted with their services. Major John Rains was the first man that ever took up arms with me in North Carolina, and the last man with me in that country, and took an active part in command in six and thirty skirmishes in N.C. (also Capt. George Rains).

At the departure of my little army I was left with three men; and in four days seventeen more came to my assistance. I made enquiry respecting the loss of the rebels in the late action, and found that the inhabitants had buried twenty-four, and that the wounded they had left behind were ninety, besides those that went off, and that my party had taken ten prisoners. Of the number of the killed was Col. Guttrell and Major Knowles, who were inveterate enemies to the loyalists.

The party we had engaged I found to have consisted of 400 Continentals under the command of Col. Maybin and General Butler's militia. In twenty-four days I found myself able to sit up, and then dispatched four of my captains, Hooker, Rains, Knight, and Lindly, to Wilmington for a supply of ammunition; and before their return I had sent out and embodied 140 men, during which time I heard of a quantity of leather which was preparing for the use of the rebel army, and was ordered for General Green's quarters at Camden. I went to the place, and finding the leather agreeable to my information, I took enough thereof to equip the company completely, and ordered the rest to be destroyed. On my return to Brush Creek, near where I had been secreted during my illness occasioned by my wounds, I sent out spies for discovery. Two of them returned in less than an hour with information of six hundred rebels who were advancing to attack me, but they proved no more than 170. These accounts disheartened a number of my men. From my being in so weak a state, they apprehended I would not be able to command them. However, they lifted me on my horse, and I formed my men then in two ranks and showed two fronts, as they appeared both in my front and rear. The fire continued for near an hour. I lost three men killed, and three badly wounded. The rebels had one killed and several wounded. Then they retreated, and rallied and attacked again, after retreating about a mile, which was so unexpected that I concluded they had been reinforced. I then retreated, but without loss, except by baggage, which they made a prize of. I then separated my men into small parties, until the arrival of the four officers I had dispatched for ammunition to Wilmington, who brought the following letter from Major Craig, with 5,000 cartridges:

WILMINGTON, 13th Oct., 1781.

"Dear Sir:

"Your letter gave me infinite satisfaction from the favourable accounts it contained of your health, and the probability of your soon being restored to that service in which you have done so much to your honour. I beg you to accept for yourself, and convey to those of your officers whom I have not yet seen, my warmest thanks for their gallantry and good behaviour. I enclose you the commission you desired for Major Rains, who I am persuaded will endeavour to answer your warm recommendations. I have been unfortunate enough to lose the list of medicines you sent for; however, I will desire the surgeon to send you such as he thinks most likely to be serviceable to you; though from his not being acquainted with your case, is all by guess. I am much concerned to find the probabilities of so many of your people suffering from want of attendance or necessaries. Nothing shall be wanting in my power, either in that respect or that of salt for their relief. I am not at liberty to explain myself in a letter, but I hope I shall very soon have it in my power to assist you with greater care than at present. The moment I returned here, and was informed of the circumstances of the stallion you mention, I determined it in your favour, and took him away from Mr. Campbell, or rather from a gentleman whom he had sold him to. He has been with my horses ever since, and never rode. I now send him to you by Capt. Liveley.

The long northerly winds has prevented any arrivals from Charleston, so that we are totally without news.

I wish I had got Mr. Burke's papers.

I am, with much regard,

Your most ob't faithful servant,   J. H. CRAIG."

The following is a copy of the letter I received of Colonel Edmond Fanning, of the King's Americans:

(Blank in the manuscript)

The names of the Officers of Cumberland county who acted under Col. McDougald, as they was commissioned in their different companies, who were with me at the taking of Hillsboro:
Archibald McDougald, Col.
Archibald McKay, Lieut.-Col.

(Another blank)

The names of the Officers of Bladen county who acted under Lt.-Col. Hector McNeal:

Hector McNeal, Lt.-Col.
John Watson, Major.

(Another blank)

The names of the Gentlemen Officers who came as Volunteers from Wilmington for recreation and to explore the country, and was at the taking of Hillsboro with me:
Alexander McCraw, Capt. of Gov. Martin's Regt.
Daniel McDonald, Lieut. of Gov. Martin's Regt.
Malcolm McKay, Ensign of Gov. Martin's Regt.
John McKenzie, Capt.
Hector McNeal.
Charles Campbell.
James Dawson.

---

*It is evident that there were two Colonels of this name, one on each side. A third, Colonel Daniel McNeill, of North Carolina, was the paternal grandfather of the late able physician and public man of Nova Scotia, Hon. D. McNeill Parker, M. L. C. No doubt the latter is the correct spelling.—A.W.S.

CHAPTER 4

SOMETIME after the receipt of the foregoing letter from Col. Edmond Fanning, I intercepted an express from Virginia bound for Gen. Greene's camp, which was at that time near the lines not far from Charleston; amongst which was Lord Cornwallis's capitulation, which I have since lost. We continued in small parties until Major Craig evacuated Wilmington, when one day I took a man with me to go for intelligence and to provide oats for the party I kept with me. When at a house I spied a party of thirty rebels coming towards said house where I was. We instantly mounted and rode off. On my return to my men, I ordered sixteen of them to mount, and went back to the house we had left, but found them gone off. I pursued them about sixteen miles, when we came up with them. We killed three of them and wounded two, whom I took prisoners. I had no loss or accident on our part.

I had now certain intelligence of Major Craig's evacuating Wilmington; and that the rebels in consequence of it had separated into small parties, and were returning toward their homes, and for the space of fourteen or fifteen days I fell in with and took more or less of them every day, during which time I had information of a Capt. Kennedy and his party, who had taken a number of horses and a quantity of household furniture. I followed him about five miles, and after a smart firing, took him and eight of his party, with the booty they had plundered. He gave intelligence that a Capt. Lopp with a party of sixty men who had been discharged by Gen. Rutherford were on their way home up the country. The said Capt. Kennedy (Cannady) all the time of our attacking Lopp stood and looked on; and as he declared that he would not make his escape, neither would he let any of his men, if we beat and drove off Capt. Lopp. I left him in a house with only two men to guard eleven, and found them all there. The guard informed me that he would not let any of his party make their escape. He proved so much to his honour that I gave him up one of his horses, saddle and bridle; and paroled him with all his men. I at this time had but thirteen men with me at a house near the road not far from where they were to pass. I mounted my men, and placed them in concealment along the road. On their coming up, I ordered them to fire and then to charge, which we did, three times, through them; they immediately dispersed through the woods; it being nearly dark, we could not tell what injury they suffered.

On the 10th of December Col. Isaacs came down from the mountains with a party of three hundred men, and formed his camp at Coxe's Mill, in the settlement I had formerly ranged in, in order to take me; where he continued nearly three months, during which time the following proclamation was issued:

"STATE OF NORTH CAROLINA.

By the Hon. Alexander Martin, Esq., Speaker of the Senate, Captain General, Governor and Commander-in-Chief in and over the said State.

Whereas divers of citizens of this State have been deluded by the wicked artifices of our enemies, and have revolted and withdrawn themselves from the faith and allegiance which, before God, they plighted to owe their country, and treacherously have taken up arms against the same; being convinced that they have been betrayed by false hopes, supported by deceit, and now find themselves deserted by our feeble and despairing enemy, and left unprotected to the vengeance of the State, to inflict those punishments due to their crimes, in tender compassion to the feelings of humanity to spare such who are willing to return, and to stay the hand of execution in the unnecessary effusion of the blood of citizens who may be reclaimed, I have thought fit to issue this my proclamation of pardon of such of the above persons who may surrender themselves before the 10th day of March next, on this express condition, that they immediately enlist in the Continental battalions, and there render a personal service for twelve months after the time of their rendezvous at headquarters, and having faithfully performed the same for the said term, it shall be deemed as having expiated their offences, and be entitled to, and be restored to the privileges of citizens. All officers finding men of this class guilty of murder, robbery, and housebreaking, to be precluded from the above not-

40

withstanding; and I do hereby require the Honourable the Judges of the Superior Courts of law, of oyer and terminer, and general jail delivery, and all officers, civil and military, within the State to take notice of this my proclamation, and govern themselves accordingly. Given under my hand and seal at arms at Halifax this 25th of December, 1781, and in the sixth year of our Independence.

ALEXANDER MARTIN.

By his Excellency's command,

JOHN HAWKINS, D. Sec'y.

"God save the State."

During Col. Isaac's stay at Coxe's Mill he ravaged the whole settlement, and burnt and destroyed a number of houses belonging to the friends of Government. They frequently applied to me privately for advice. I recommended it to them, if possible, to remain neutral, and make their peace; as it was entirely out of my power to protect or relieve them. A Capt. Stinson of this party took one of my men named David Jackson, *and hung him up without ceremony.* A few days before Col. Isaac's departure from Coxe's Mills, he sent out notice for the friends of Government to meet him, and he would give them protection agreeable to proclamation; but on their assembling, he made them prisoners of war, and marched them under a strong guard to Salisbury gaol. Not many days after, they broke out and knocking down the sentinels, made their escape except one, who was shot in the attempt.

Two Captains in each county were appointed by Col. Isaacs, on his leaving Coxe's Mill, to keep the friends of Government down; and were going with their own men continually through the country.

During all this time I was in the woods, and kept moving with a small party as occasion required. One evening I had assembled thirty men at a friend's house, and sent out spies; they soon returned with accounts of a party of rebels within four miles of us, distressing and plundering our friends. We immediately set forward to render our assistance, and got within half a mile of them. I then sent out to get information how they were situated, and receiving intelligence by break of day came upon them. We retook seven horses, which they had carried off, with a large quantity of baggage. We wounded two of them mortally and several slightly; we came off without injury, except two horses wounded. The day following we pursued them to Cumberland county, and on my way I burnt Capt.

41

Coxe's house, and his father's. I had also two skirmishes and killed two of the rebel party. On my return to Little River I heard of a Capt. Golson who had been distressing the loyalists, and went in search of him myself, but unfortunately I did not meet him, but fell in with one of his men, who had been very assiduous in assisting the rebels. I killed him. I mounted a man of my own on his horse and returned back. I then took Capt. Currie and the man of my own before mentioned, and went with a design of burning Capt. Golson's house, which I did; and also two others. In my way I fell in with a man *who had been very anxious to have some of my men executed.* I sent him word to moderate and he should have nothing to fear, but if he persisted, I would certainly kill him. He took no notice of this, but persisted for several months, and on observing me that day, he attempted to escape; but I shot him.

Two days after Capt. Walker joined me, which made four of us, and hearing that one Thompson, a rebel magistrate, had taken up a horse belonging to one of my men, I went to claim him; he gave him up without hesitation, and upon examining what arms he had, he owned to one rifle, which I took from him; he also informed me that the rebels were willing to make peace with me on my own terms, and would allow me any limited bounds I would require, provided I would not be troublesome to them. I therefore concluded after consulting Capt. Walker and Currie, to demand the following terms, which I forwarded by a prisoner I had taken; and in order to convince them that my intentions were sincere, I released him for that purpose, *though he had been the means of murdering several.*

Terms required by Col. David Fanning from Gov. Burke, forwarded to him by Lawyer Williams and Capt. Ramsay, of 1st battalion of North Carolina Continentals:

1. That every friend of the Government shall be allowed to return to their respective homes unmolested.

2. That they shall be under no restrictions of doing, or causing to be done, any thing prejudicial to his Majesty's service.

3. That they shall not be under any obligation to act in any public station, or ever to take up arms, or be compelled to do anything injurious to his Majesty's good government.

4. That they shall not pay, or cause to be paid, any taxes or money so levied by your laws during the continuance of the present war, to support your army by their industry. If these terms are granted, I request that they may be immediately conveyed to me at my quarters by a flag of truce, appointed for that purpose, and by

such officers as I can rely upon, from your hands and seals.

If these terms are not granted you may depend upon my sword being continually unsheathed; as I am determined I will not leave one of your old offenders alive that has injured his Majesty's Government, and friends who would have been of service to your country in a future day, and I do hereby recommend it to you to govern yourselves accordingly.

Jan. 7th, 1782.   DAVID FANNING,

Colonel.
JOSEPH CURRIE,
STEPHEN WALKER,
Captains.

To Mr. James Williams and Capt. Matthew Ramsay.
To be forwarded by them to the Commander in Chief for the time being, Hillsboro district.

I received the following answer from Lawyer Williams:

CHATHAM, Jan. 8th, 1782.

SIR,—I received yours by Mr. Riggin at the Court House on Sunday last, and immediately wrote to Gen. Butler on the subject of your surrender, as mentioned in yours. His answer is that he cannot receive you himself but will directly write to the Governor, and as soon as he receives his answer, he will transmit it to Maj. Griffith, who will send it to Winsor Pearce's on Deep River. If I obtain liberty, I will bring it myself. In the meantime I would recommend a moderate conduct as the best step to bring matters to an accommodation. The bearer, Mr. Riggin, has executed the trust you reposed in him; I therefore hope you will restore to him his property. *For your civility to me when I was a prisoner, I will do anything I can in honour.* Concerning your surrender, Col. Ray and Col. McDougald have surrendered and gone to Charleston. I am informed by Col. Thackston I am exchanged with a number of other prisoners at Charleston under a cartel which is renewed. You may depend as soon as I get the Governor's answer, you shall know it.

I am, Sir, your most obedient servant,

JAMES WILLIAMS

COL. DAVID FANNING.

I also received another letter from Capt. Ramsay by another conveyance:

Jan. 8th, 1782.

SIR,—I saw a letter to Mr. Williams and observed what you say concerning my case. As to breaking my parole, that I am clear of; as Major Craig a few days before he left Wilmington sent a party of

43

dragoons to where we were paroled at the Sound and ordered us under the main guard, whence I made my escape; which I am certain you will not blame me for, as you are well acquainted with my honour; when I was taken prisoner, I had it in my power to escape many a time, but as long as I was treated like a gentleman, or agreeably to the rules of war, I would rather suffer death than forfeit my honour. I observe what you say concerning your parole; for *the kind treatment I received at your hands, you may rely on it, anything Mr. Williams or myself can do for you in honour* shall not be wanting. Your letter I understand is transmitted to the Governor, who I make no doubt will comply with your request. For my part I wish for nothing else but peace.

I am, Sir, your humble servant,

MATTHEW RAMSAY.

I lay neutral until I got further accounts and on the 15th Jan., 1782, Messrs. Williams, Clark, and Burns, were kind enough to wait on me at Mr. Winsor Pearce's with respect to my former proposals which I had requested of them, with the letter as follows:

15th Jan., 1782.

SIR,—Agreeable to your request I have received order to offer you a parole on the terms you desired, thirty miles east and west, fifteen miles north and south. Hammond Coxe's mill to be the centre of your bounds. Should you incline to go to Charleston at a future day, let me know it, and I will endeavour to get you that liberty when I see the Governor.

You mentioned being waylaid; you may be assured that I know nothing of it. Mr. Williams, Mr. Clark and John Burns are the gentlemen that are kind enough to wait upon you with this flag, and a blank parole for you to sign, and they will give you a certificate for your security against any of the American troops to remain as prisoner of war in the bounds specified. You may rely on it, nothing dishonourable shall be done on my part; and I have the greatest reason to believe that you will act on the same principles. No inhabitants of this county shall be molested, either in person or property, who have not been guilty of wilful murder, or plundering; it is the duty of every honest man to bring all such to justice in order to restore harmony and peace once more to our country.

I am your obedient humble servant,

MATTHEW RAMSAY.

To Col. David Fanning
per flag.

Also the following letter was left at Mr. Pearce's by the three gentlemen before mentioned:

TUESDAY MORNING.

SIR,—Agreeable to Capt. Ramsay's letter left for you, we came up to Mr. Pearce's when we made no doubt of seeing you. I have seen his instructions to parole you, and you may depend no trap is meant for you, to any of our knowledge. Ray and McDougald were received in the same manner, and no man offered to molest them. Our orders were to have returned last night, and the Light Horse under the command of Capt. Ramsay kept back until our return; therefore we cannot possibly stay any longer. If you incline to accept the terms offered, which Capt. Ramsay cannot alter, you will meet us at Baalam Thompson's with as many of your men as you please, such as can be received according to the terms you propose, and are your obedient servants.

JAMES WILLIAMS,
A. CLARK,
JNO. BURNS.

TO COL. DAVID FANNING.

In the course of this correspondence endeavouring to make peace, I had reason to believe they did not intend to be as good as their words; as three of their people followed Capt. Linley of mine, who had moved to Wittoguar, and cut him to pieces with their swords. I was immediately informed of it, and kept a look-out for them. Five days after their return, I took two of them and hung them, by way of retaliation, both on a limb of one tree, they being deserters from the British (Col. Hamilton's Regiment); the third made his escape. After this Col. Alstine, who was a prisoner of war at this time, came to me at Gen. Butler's request, to know if I was willing to come to any terms. I asked the reason why the Governor had not answered my letter, and what was the cause of their behaviour to Capt. Linley. I then, with a number of my officers, sat down and wrote the following letter to General Butler:

"SIR,—On Friday, the 7th of January last, I wrote to Mr. Williams the terms I was willing to come under; he wrote for answer that he could not comply with my terms until he had the approbation of the Governor. On Wednesday, the 11th January, a flag was to meet me at Winsor Pearce's with a letter. But on its approach it was waylaid by Capt. Golston with a party of men, which had more the appearance of treachery than a wish for peace, had not the gentleman (Mr. Baalam Thompson) acted as honourable; for the minute he arrived

45

he let me know it, and declared himself innocent. This gave me reason to think he would act with honour. Still on the 15th January, Messrs. Williams, Clark, and Burns, the three gentlemen that were kind enough to wait upon me, with a blank parole, and letter from Capt. Ramsay—who mentioned in his letter that my request was granted by the Governor; in the meantime, the gentlemen waiting on me at the place appointed, there came around a company from the Hawfields, commanded by Capt. Scorely, which plainly and evidently appeared to me there was nothing but treachery meant." On Sunday, the 10th of February, I fell in the rear of Capt. Colestons and Capt. Hinds, and following their trail, came on them at dark. After some firing that night I rode off, and came on them next morning, and we came upon terms of peace till I could write to their superior officer, for which I consulted my officers, and we joined hand and heart to comply with the terms hereunder written.

"We, the Subscribers, do acknowledge ourselves subjects to his Britannic Majesty, as you are well assured of our fidelity, zeal, and loyalty to his Majesty's government, as it has been daily the case that we have been destroying one another's property to support and uphold our opinions, and we are hereby willing to come to a cession of arms, not under six months, nor exceeding twelve; conditions underwritten.

1. Our request is from Cumberland, twenty miles N. & S., and thirty miles E. & W., to be totally clear of your Light Horse.

2nd. Request is for every man that has been in actual arms, in a permanent manner, in order to establish a British Government (except those who have deserted from a regular troop that has voluntarily listed themselves), them we do obligate to deliver up, and each and every man that are at liberty, shall have a right to withdraw themselves in said district.

3rd. If any of our men should go out of said district to plunder, or distress, or murder any of the American party, we will, by information made of me, Major Rains, or any of the Captains, return their names (if the request is granted); they shall immediately be apprehended and sent by any officer appointed by you to be tried by your own laws.

4th If any of your party shall be caught plundering, stealing or murdering, or going private paths with arms, signifying as if they were for mischief, these are to be left to our pleasure to deal with as we see cause agreeable to our laws. All public roads to be travelled by any person or company unmolested if he behave himself as becomes an honest man, or any army or company or waggons keeping the public roads.

5th. Every person that has been in actual arms in manner aforesaid, in order to support or establish a British Government, shall not be interrupted of their arms, provisions, person or property. If any one residing within the said district who are subjects to the States that you should want provisions or any other article from, by sending to either of the officers that I shall appoint for that purpose or use, we will send a sufficient guard to see them safe in and out unmolested. Quakers excepted from anything whatever.

6th. That I will not in the meantime disturb or distress any person or persons abiding by your laws in said district. All back plundering shall be void, as it is impossible to replace or restore all the plunder on either side.

7th. Our request is to have free trade with any port with waggons, or on horseback without arms; with a pass from any appointed officer for salt or any other necessaries and use, except the two Coxe's mills, to be free from any incumbrance of all armies belonging to the Americans.

8th. Any of my men that has been returned a Continental without taking the bounty, that has been in actual service as above mentioned, shall return in said district.

9th. If our request is granted as above written I request it may be sent to me by 8th of March, as I may forward my further determinations; if I cannot have any request granted, I shall exact and point out every feasible measure in order to suppress every person in arms against his Britannic Majesty. I am your most obedient humble servant.

Given under my hand at arms as aforesaid.

DAVID FANNING, *Col. Com. Loyal Militia.*
JOHN RAINS, *MAJOR LOYAL MILITIA.*
WILLIAM RAINS, *Captain.*
JOHN CAGLE, *Captain.*
WM. PRICE, *Captain.*
ABNER SMALLY, *Captain.*
JACOB MANNIES, *Lieutenant.*
To John Butler, Gen'l of Hillsboro District
Pr favour of Col. Philip Alstine.
A copy of a letter received from Gen. Butler:
MOUNT PLEASANT, 5th March, 1782.
DEAR SIR:

Your letter of 26th of last month was handed to me last night. I have obswerved the contents. Had you proposed that you and the men now in actual service with you would have taken a parole to some certain bounds, until you could have been sent to Charleston to be exchanged, I should have entered on that business. But as your propositions are many, and some of them uncustomary in like cases, I conceive it out of my power. However, his Excellency Governor Burke is now at Halifax, and I will send him your letter with the proposals to him by express. This is now the 5th day of March; of course, it must be several days after the 8th before his answer can come to hand; in the meantime it may be as well to postpone the desperate measures you have in contemplation.

I am your obedient servant,

JOHN BUTLER, *B.G. for*
Hillsboro District.

P.S.—If you would not choose to be confined to bounds any length of time, it might be contrived so that you might be sent off immediately under an escort of my appointing to General Greene. He has promised me to have all such exchanged which I send to his quarters.

JOHN BUTLER, B.G.

About the 7th of March, 1782, Capt. Walker and Currie of the Loyal Militia fell in with a party of rebels and came to an engagement, and fired for some time, till the rebels had fired all their ammunition, and then wished to come to terms of peace between each party; and no plundering, killing or murdering should be committed by either party or side, which was to be concluded upon by each Colonel for such certain limited bounds which were to be agreed upon by each Colonel; and if they could not agree, each party was to lie neutral until matters were made known respecting the terms which they wished to agree upon; soon after which my men came to me and informed what they had done; we received the rebel Col. Balfour's answer, that "there was no resting place for a Tory's foot upon the earth." He also immediately sent out his party, and on the 10th I saw the same company coming to a certain house where we were fiddling and dancing. We immediately prepared ourselves in readiness to receive them, their number being twenty-seven and our number only seven; we immediately mounted our horses, and went some little distance from the house and commenced a fire, for some considerable time; night coming on they retreated, and left the ground.

On the 12th of March my men being all properly equipped, assembled together in order to give them a small scourge, which we set out for. On Balfour's plantation, where we came upon him, he endeavoured to make his escape; but we soon prevented him, having fired at him and wounded him. The first ball he received was through one of his arms, and ranged through his body; the other through his neck; which put an end to his commiting any more ill deeds.

We also wounded another of his men. We then proceeded to their Colonel's (Collier), belonging to said county of Randolph; on our way we burnt several rebel houses and caught several prisoners, the night coming on and the distance to said Collier's was so far, that it was late before we got there. He made his escape, having received three balls through his shirt, but I took care to destroy the whole of his plantation. I then pursued our route, and came to one Capt. John Bryan's, another rebel officer. I told him if he would come out of the house, I would give him a parole, which he refused, saying that he had taken a parole from Lord Cornwallis, swearing by God, he had broken that and that he would also break our Tory parole. With that I immediately ordered the house to be set on fire, which was instantly done, and as soon as he saw the flames of the fire increasing, he called out to me, and desired me to spare his house for his wife's and children's sake, and he would walk out with his arms in his hands. I immediately answered him, that if he walked out his house should be saved for his wife and children. He came out, and when he came out he said, "Here, damn you, here I am." With that he received two balls, one through his head and one through his body; he came out with his gun cocked, and sword at the same time.

Next day I proceeded to one Major Dugin's house, or plantation, and I destroyed all his property, and all the rebel officers' property in the settlement for the distance of forty miles.

On our way I caught a commissary from Salisbury who had some of my men prisoners and almost perished them, and wanted to hang some of them. I carried him immediately to a certain tree, *where they had hung one of my men by the name of Jackson*, and delivered him up to some of my men, whom he had treated ill when prisoners; and they immediately hung him. After hanging fifteen minutes they cut him down. In the meantime there was about 300 rebels who had embodied themselves and came after us; on account of the rainy weather our guns would not fire on either side. We were obliged to retreat, on account of their numbers being so much superior. We had received no damage.

* Col. David Fanning, of North Carolina, was one of the most remarkable characters developed by the American Revolution. His own narrative of his sufferings, exploits, marvellous adventures and hairbreath escapes during the war has for years past been an object of quest by writers and students of American and Colonial history.—A.W.S.

CHAPTER 5

ABOUT the 8th of April, a certain Capt. Williams came into the settlement and sent an old woman to me, to inform me that he had arrived from Governor Burke that instant, and had come in order to see me; by her description I and my little party immediately met him, and he informed me that he had come to know if I was willing to come upon those terms I had already presented; and requested to have from under my own hand a true copy of them, and that Governor Burke would do everything in his power to have the same agreed upon by his Council and Assembly; for which purpose the said Williams was sent from the Governor. He also told me that the Governor had said that anything I should do, or cause to be done, from the character he had heard from the British at Charleston, that he had not the least doubt they would assent to any proceedings I should undertake to do; he wished to make peace with me; and also saying if I was taken prisoner and killed, that 100 would certainly lose their lives for it, and he looked upon it much better to come upon terms of peace—that he heard in Charleston that I was killed, which occasioned him to run away from Charleston; upon which I gave him a copy of the articles which I wished to comply to; with which he ordered the Light Horse to depart to their different stations till they had received orders from the Governor and Council.

As I was obliged to lay neutral until I received their answer, which was to be upon terms of honour between both sides, with which the different captains commanding the Light Horse wrote to me respecting the same; which appears by the following letters:

SIR,—I received a few lines this day from Capt. Edward Williams, informing me that you and he had come down yesterday, and signified that you and he are upon terms of compromising matters, on condition that I will stop the Country Light Horse from pursuing you. You may rest assured that it is my desire to be at peace with all men. Capt. Riddle and his company are at the Court House. I have ordered him to stand there until further orders, and will send after Capt. Golston and desire him in also. I shall set off this morning to the Assembly, and if it is in my power to do or cause anything to be done that shall cause peace and harmony over the land, you may rest assured I will do my best, and second Capt. Williams, though he gave me no account of your proposals; and am

With respect your humble servant,

ROGER GRIFFITH, Major.

April 9th, 1782.

To Col. David Fanning.

CAMP AT MR. CARR'S, Apr. 10, 1782.

SIR,—I received orders from Major Griffith concerning some terms between him and you and shall withdraw my men and Capt. Golston's as we are both together, and will not proceed any further after apprehending you or yours, unless you come into our county doing mischief, until further orders.

From your humble servant,

JOSEPH ROSUR.

To Col. David Fanning.

Hoping you nor yours will not interrupt any of the inhabitants of Chatham until matters are further settled.

WILLIAM GOLSTON.

SIR,—I received your letter, which gives me great satisfaction to hear that you and some of the officers have come upon terms of peace, which is all I would crave; but I should be glad with one of the officers in company to meet you and have some conversation together, and be upon honour, and if we can come upon terms agreeable to both, I should immediately march my company home; so I shall be at Mr. Mullins this evening at two o'clock; and if you can meet and converse across the river, or any other place you will choose.

I am, sir, your obedient

THOMAS DOUGAN,
Captain of Light Horse.

April 12th, 1782.

To Col. David Fanning.

April 17th, 1782.

SIR,—I, as an officer in behalf of the State of North Carolina, have turned out in order to suppress any persons disturbing the peace of said State; but when I arrived at Deep River, I understood that you and Capts. Williams and Dougan were about to make a treaty of peace (which I approved of very well), and withdrew my troop towards home. But to my surprise, on my way I understood that your men were robbing the peaceful and inoffensive people of Cane Creek and Rocky River, which wicked conduct, and the great desire I had for the welfare of my country, induced me to stay a little longer, and endeavour to stop such robbery. I therefore wish to inform you that I did not pretend with any view of making you any way dishonourable, but many persons not owing a true allegiance to the laws of this State are running at large and call you their officer. As I hope you are a gentleman, and will not protect any vagabond, I will thank you to let me know every particular of your treaty, or what bounds you have; and upon the honour of a gentleman I will not interrupt any person within said bounds that is of good character with you. I would recommend that you order Joseph Currie and Blair to return the widow Dixon's property, which they robbed her of, and I will not write to the Governor concerning it, as you want peace. He would think very little of your honour if he heard that your men were robbing his people after you had petitioned to him.

I am, sir, in behalf of the State,

EDWARD GUIN, *Captain.*

To Col. David Fanning.

About the 18th of April Capt. Williams came to me again at Fort Creek, and informed me that the original articles of treaty had been laid before the Governor and Assembly, and they were upon a conclusion of granting me the terms I wanted; but were prevented by a Colonel who came from over the mountains and was one of the Assembly, who did everything against it. Their objections were the articles respecting the Continental soldiers to be taken off, and also that they could not think of allowing any passports for any of the friends of Government to have any correspondence or connections with the British. Every other article they were willing to grant. Their Assembly continued on the business for three days, as Mr. Williams informed me. My answer was that I would forfeit my life before I would withdraw any one of the articles that I had presented, as I still wished to hold the same connection with the British as formerly; I likewise told him, that I understood that they had picked out twenty-four of their best horses and men from Virginia in order to pursue me, and my answer to Mr. Williams was that they might do their best, and be damned, as I was fully determined to still support my integrity, and to exert myself in behalf of the King and country more severely than ever I did. With this Mr. Williams departed.

I then set out for Chatham, where I learned that a wedding was to be that day. On my way I took one prisoner before I came to the house. There being but five of us, we immediately surrounded the house in full charge. I ordered them immediately out of the house. Three of my men went into the house and drove them all out one by one. I caused them all to stand in a row to examine them, to see if I knew any of them that were bad men.* I found one, by the name of William Doudy, concealed upstairs. One of my men fired at him as he was running from one house to the other; he received the ball in his shoulder. I then having my pistols in my hand, discharged them both at his breast, with which he fell, and that night expired. I then paroled the rest on the 25th.

I concluded within myself that it was better for me to try and settle myself, being weary of the disagreeable mode of living I had borne with for some considerable time; and for the many kindnesses and the civility of a gentleman who lived in the settlement of Deep River, I was induced to pay my *addresses* to his daughter, a young lady of sixteen years of age. The day of marriage being appointed, on making it known to my people, Capt. William Hooker and Captain William Carr agreed to be married with me. They both left me to make themselves and their intended wives ready, and the day before we were to be coupled, the rebels before mentioned, with those good horses, came upon them. Capt. Hooker's horse being tied so fast he could not get him loose, they caught him and murdered him on the spot. Myself and Capt. Carr were married and kept two days' merriment. The rebels thought they were sure of me then; however, I took my wife and concealed her in the woods with Capt. Carr's; and caused an oration to be put out that I was gone to Charleston. In order to be convinced, the rebels sent a man in as a spy, with two letters from Gen. Leslie with instructions for me to enlist men for the service, which I knew was forged, in order to betray me, and from the person or commanding officer of the rebel Light Horse. The following is one of which I gave Gen. Leslie, that had his name signed on it:

CHARLESTON, 20th Jan., 1782.

DEAR COLONEL,—

Although I have not as yet the happiness of being acquainted with you, yet I can but applaud you very much for your spirited conduct and activity. The only objection I have to your conduct is your being too strenuous with those who have been subjects to his Majesty, and whom the rebels have overcome and forced them to comply with their laws. If you would let them alone, the severity of the rebels would cause them to return to their allegiance again. But, sir, since you have made so brave a stand already, pray stand steadfast to the end, and we shall be well rewarded at the last. Try to spirit up your men, and enlist, if possible, three hundred men this spring, ready to join three hundred more; which shall be put under your command, and you be Brigadier-General of them, and as many more as you can get. We shall, I hope, in the month of May land 1,300 troops in North Carolina, 300 for you to join your corps, 1,600 in the whole, to act upon the defensive until you are reinforced.

Keep good discipline among your troops, and keep out fellows who will do nothing but plunder from amongst your people. They are but false dependence, and will not fight, but only corrupt good men. Every man you enlist for twelve months shall receive ten guineas and a full suit of clothes as soon as we land our troops, and they appear under your command ready for action. I can assure you, 'tis your fame and worthy actions has, through and by Major Craig given, reached his Majesty's ears, and I expect perhaps by the next packet boat you will get a genteel present from our gracious Sovereign. So hoping that you will be in the way of your duty, I will take leave of you, without mentioning your name, or subscribing mine, lest this might miscarry—the man who is entrusted with the care of this dares not at present be seen in it, but a friend, and send it to the man it is directed to.

Sir, yours,

To Col. Fanning in No. Ca.

A letter from the traitor who brought these two letters from Gen. Leslie:

DEAR SIR,—

I would come to see you myself, but am afraid of the rebel Light Horse. I have a great many things to acquaint you with and a good deal of good news, but dare not write for fear of miscarriage. If you have any desire of seeing me you must come soon, nay, instantly.

Don't let the bearer know the contents of the letters—the fewer trusted the better. In the meantime,

I am your friend and servant,

JOSEPH WILSON.

April 29th, 1782.

To Col. Fanning.

My answer was in Major Rains' name as follows:

SIR,—I am very sorry to think that there is so many damned foolish rebels in the world, as to think Col. Fanning would be ever deceived by such damned infernal writing as I have received from you. Col. Fanning is gone to Charleston, and is not to return here till he comes with forces sufficient to defend this part of the country, and I would have you to disband, and be gone immediately; for if I ever hear of any of your people coming with anything of the sort, I will come and kill him myself. I am in behalf of his Majesty's armies,

JOHN RAINS,
Major of the Loyal Militia.

To Jos. Wilson.

On the 1st of May, 1782, I heard a waggon going in the road; I imagined she was going down to market, as I heard of a number of waggons which were to proceed down with liquors to the market. On the 2nd I mounted and pursued the waggon which I heard the day before, and as I was about setting out for Charleston I concluded to have a frolic with my old friends before we parted. After riding about ten miles I overtook the said waggon, which belonged to a certain man who had been taken prisoner and paroled by the British, and had broken his parole. In the meantime, I was examining his papers I set a sentinel over him. He, knowing himself guilty, expected nothing but death. He took an opportunity and sprung upon my own riding mare, and went off with my saddle, holsters, pistols, and all my papers of any consequence to me. We fired two guns at him; he received two balls through his body, but it did not prevent him from sitting the saddle, and he made his escape. I took the other man and caused him to take me to the man's plantation, where I took his wife, and three negro boys, and eight head of horses. I kept his wife in the woods for three days, and sent the other man to see if he would deliver up my mare and property containing my papers, for which he wrote me the following answer or letter:

SIR,—Col. Fanning, I hope that you do not blame me for what I did. Hoping you will have mercy on me, as I am wounded, and let my wife come to me. Your mare shall be returned to you without fail. Your mare I don't crave, and I hope you don't covet mine. I beg that you will have pity on my wife and children. The negroes and horses I am willing you shall keep until you get your mare. I have sent to a doctor. But the mare will be back to-night. No more, but you may depend upon my word.

ANDREW HUNTER.

To Col. David Fanning.

I also received the following letter from Edward Williams on the subject of the mare:

SIR,—These few lines comes to let you know that I have this day seen Mr. Hunter, and he is badly wounded and desires you would let his wife come to him immediately. As to the rest of the property, you are welcome to keep until such time's you get your mare returned, which will be as soon as possible, as she has gone at this time after the doctor. But she shall be returned to you with all speed as soon as she returns. Mr. Hunter is also very ill.

I am your obedient humble servant,

EDWARD WILLIAMS.

Col. David Fanning.

On the 7th of May, finding I could see no opportunity of getting my mare, notwithstanding she was one of my principal creatures, and a mare I set great store by, and gave one hundred and ten guineas for, I was obliged to let loose all his horses except one, as they were of no account to me in the situation I was in; the negroes I kept. I then proceeded on to Major Gainer's truce land on Pedee in South Carolina, where he had made a truce with the rebels some time before, and I continued there until June, when I left my wife, horses and negroes, and then, as I was entirely a stranger to the situation of the country and roads, I was obliged to procure a pilot to proceed to Charleston; I could not get one for less than twenty guineas. After my departure I fell in with the rebel dragoons commanded by Col. Ballie, from Virginia. I was with them for about an hour; and informed them that we were some of the rebel party then on our way to General Marion's headquarters. They never discovered us as otherwise than such, it being in the dusk of the evening. We fell into the rear, and went into the woods and struck our camp and promised them we would see them next morning. However, we proceeded on that night and arrived at Herald's point on the 17th of June, and immediately procured a passage to Charleston, where I immediately applied for a flag to send after Mrs. Fanning and

57

property. The flag had left Charleston two days, when she came in, as Major Gainer had applied to General Marion for a pass for her to proceed to Charleston, but would not let her have any of our property, or even a negro to wait on her.

In a short time loyalists that had got into Charleston from different parts of the world, hearing that the Southern Colonies were to be evacuated by the British forces, called a meeting to point out some measures to try to hold some foothold in the country, until we had got some part payment for our property which we were obliged to leave if we left the country. Handbills were struck and stuck up through the town for the loyalists to choose their representatives to represent our situation and the desire we had to support ourselves and property. It was proposed that twenty-five gentlemen should be chosen a committee for that purpose. The days were appointed to take votes. I was chosen amongst others; and drew up a petition and sent to Sir Guy Carleton, Commander-in-Chief, praying the liberty of keeping the town and artillery, as they stood on the works, and despatched two gentlemen off with our petition; our request was not granted. I have hereunto set forth the names of the gentlemen representatives:

Col. Ballingall, Jas. Johnston, Esq.; Robert Williams, Esq.; Lt.-Col. Dupont, Col. Robt. Wm. Powell, Col. Gray, John Gailliard, Esq.; Col. Cassels, John Rose, Col. Pearson, Maj. Wm. Greenwood, Col. Philips, Maj. Gabriel Capers, Col. Hamilton, Lt.-Col. Thos. Inglis, Wm. Carson, John Hopton, Esq.; Dr. Wm. Charles Wells, Robt. Johnston, Esq.; Col. Thomas Edgehill, John Champniss, Andrew Millar, Esq.; Col. Samuel Bryan, Col. David Fanning, Doctor Baron.

I remained in Charleston until the 5th of September, and my horses having got recruited, and one of my negroes having made his way good through the country, came down to me; I then set out for the country again, on account of my misfortune of losing my mare, which was of great value to me. I went up to the settlement again, to the man I sent to Hunter before, and he informed me that Hunter refused five negroes for the mare and would not return her. He also went to where I left one of the negroes and took him and sent him over the mountains to keep him out of my way. I continued about in the settlement until the 22nd of the month, trying to get her, but was disappointed in my hopes. Knowing that Charleston was to be evacuated, I was obliged to return; and as I was on my way, I understood my mare was at a certain place, about 125 miles from

Charleston, being about half the distance from where I then was toward Charleston. I instantly pursued on my journey to the place where she then was. I came within a mile of where I heard she was, and my riding horse was so particularly known, I sent a man up to the house and he was known, and they directed us the wrong way, and immediately sent word to where my mare was. I found out we were wrong; and took through the woods and to a house within a half a mile, where they had word of my coming and were making ready to go to their assistance, but seeing us come up, he immediately left his horse, and was running off through a field, and turned round and presented his piece and snapped, but she missed fire; with this, I ordered one of my men to fire at him, who shot him through the body, and despatched his presence from this world. The other two men that was at the house that did not run, informed me that they had received word of my coming a half an hour before I arrived, and also that there were men lying in ambush ready to attack me. With this, the man who had my mare went off with her, and having only two men and my negro that set out with me from Charleston, also two little negroes that I had for my mare, I thought it was my best way to proceed to Charleston, and on the 28th September I arrived at Charleston, where the shipping was ready for me to embark for St. Augustine.

The following is a Proclamation which I got when I was out in the country, nailed to Coxe's Mill:

STATE OF NORTH CAROLINA:

By his Excellency Alexander Martin, Esq., Governor, Captain-General and Commander-in-Chief in and over the said State.

A PROCLAMATION

Whereas divers citizens of this State have withdrawn themselves from their allegiance and joined the enemy of this and the United States, seduced by their wicked artifices, now find their hopes, supported by deceit, totally blasted and left unprotected to the Justice of their country ready to inflict those just punishments due to their crimes. But in compassion to such who are truly penitent and to stop the further effusion of the blood of citizens who may be reclaimed, by and with the advice and consent of the Council of State I have thought proper to issue this my proclamation of pardon to all such of the above persons who shall within ten days after the date hereof surrender themselves to any commanding officer of any troops of the State or any of the United States acting in conjunction with the same, on this express condition that they renew

59

the oath of allegiance and enter into one of the Continental battalions of this State and there serve twelve months after the time of their rendezvous, which service being faithfully performed shall expiate their offences and entitle them to the restoration of their property and every other privilege of a citizen, precluding all those guilty of murder, robbing, house-breaking and crimes not justifiable by the laws of war from the above pardon, notwithstanding notifying all such persons that unless they surrender at the time aforesaid, those taken prisoners shall be deemed prisoners of war, and liable to exchange except as above provided. The enemy will exchange the same, otherwise they shall be subjected to the penalties of the said law which will be inflicted upon them.

By Order of his Excellency ALEXANDER MARTIN, ESQ.,

BENNETT CROFTON, *Major,*
States Legion.

June the 15th, 1782.

During my absence from Charleston, the loyalists were signing to go under my directions to East Florida, and as soon as I came to town I ordered them all to get on board, and on the 6th of November I went on board the transport ship, the *New Blessing,* commanded by Thomas Craven, where I continued on board the said transport for eight days before she set out for St. Augustine. Arrived the 17th said month, where we came to anchor, and there laid eight days more; at the expiration of that time I went on shore and three days after had my property landed, about twenty-seven miles distance from St. Augustine, upon the Matanzeys, where I had some thought of settling. I continued there for some time and from thence proceeded to Halifax River, being about fifty-five miles from St. Augustine. There I undertook to settle myself and to make a crop, thinking to begin the world anew, being tolerably well provided for with negroes.

In the last of February I met Major Andrew Deavoce, who was beating up for volunteers to go to take New Providence. I also agreed to join him and took a copy of the Articles and went home and raised thirty young men for that expedition, and had them in readiness to embark and waited for Major Deavoce arrival at the inlet of Halifax, until I heard he was gone. A true copy of the original is hereunto set forth:

Articles of Agreement between Major Deavoce and the Volunteers, for an expedition immediately against New Providence:

Article 1st. I do engage on my part to furnish the men with provisions, arms and ammunition for the expedition.

2nd. That the men shall be altogether under my command and not to be transferred to any other after the expedition, and that they rendezvous on the fifteenth of this month in town, and be ready to go on board on three hours' notice being given them.

3rd. That all or any of the men who shall desire to settle in that country after the reduction of it shall be provided with land.

4th. That all prizes taken by land or sea shall be equally divided among the officers and men according to their respective ranks, first deducting the expense of the expedition.

5th. That in case of mutiny or disobedience of orders the man or party concerned shall forfeit the whole of their prize money and be subject to confinement for the offence according to the nature of the crime.

6th. That a certain number of dead shares shall be reserved for the support of all wounded men, widows and orphans of men that may unfortunately fall on this expedition. Ten dead shares shall be at the disposal of Capt. Wheeler and myself for deserving men.

7th. That the person who raises the most men shall be second in command, and I do engage if any person or persons should not be willing to remain in the Bahamas to furnish them with a passage to Jamaica or back to St. Augustine.

ST. AUGUSTINE, 3rd of March, 1783.

We who have subscribed our names as under, do hereby agree to go with Major Andrew Deavoce on the within expedition as volunteers, complying with the within rules and to hold ourselves in readiness for embarking on said expedition on the fifteenth of this inst. Either of us refusing to comply with the above and within rules and articles shall forfeit to Major Andrew Deavoce, his heirs or assigns, the sum of ten pounds sterling money of Great Britain.

After this I began to notice my negroes beginning to get sick and six of them died. Some time after I went to St. Augustine I was taken sick and lay at the point of death for three weeks. I then began at last to walk, and one day I went to my field to where I had a young negro about twenty years of age at work. I took my rifle with me as usual; I set her down by a tree. I felt very sick and weak; I laid myself down on some grass and my negro took up my rifle and came within ten yards and set himself down and took aim at my head, but luckily the ball missed my head about one inch, but it split my hat. I then got up and went towards him, when he ran at me with the gun and struck at my head. But I fended it off with my arms. He however broke the stock, forward of the lock. I knowing myself weak, I turned and ran sixty yards, but found myself not able to run. I got my feet entangled in some vines and unfortunately fell, and he came to me and with the barrel of my rifle he struck at me many times. I lay on my back and fended his strokes with my heels until he had knocked all the bottoms of my feet to blisters. His great eagerness to kill me put him much out of wind. I accidentally got hold of the gun barrel and he tried to bite my hand for some time. During the time of his trying to bite me, I knocked all his fore teeth out. At last he run for his hoe and made one stroke at me and broke one of the bones of my left arm. But I took the opportunity of giving him a stroke on his temple with which I brought him down. I then mended my blows until he appeared to be dead. As I had got him down my wife came in sight of me, and he lay for some time to appearance dead, until two men came to me as they had heard me hollowing. He at length come to and walked home. I confined him to take him to justice. He lived till the next day, and at the same hour the next he was sitting, eating, and all of a sudden he fell dead.

In a short time after I heard peace was proclaimed and for the loyalists to send an estimation of their losses and services; also, that the Province of East Florida was to be immediately evacuated, and the ships came to take all the provincial troops to Nova Scotia; the officers that were acquainted with me insisted for me to go with them, but I had not time to get my family and property to town in time, and as it was uncertain where I should go to, some of the gentlemen officers desired to give me a certificate to let my services be known, let me go where I would—a true copy of which is hereunto set forth:

EAST FLORIDA.

We whose names are hereunto subscribed, do hereby certify that Col. David Fanning, late of the Province of No. Ca., acted in the station of Colonel of Militia of that Province, and was of the greatest service to his Majesty in suppressing the rebels during the late rebellion in North America, and that he is worthy of every loyal subject both for his valour and good conduct; that after he with his men took the town of Hillsborough, dispersed the rebel council, and took a great number of prisoners, he was on that day wounded in the left arm—that finding the town of Wilmington evacuated by the British troops, and his wound not yet well, he, for the safety of his people, divided them into small parties, and continued a long

62

time in the back woods; that after many skirmishes in North Carolina, in the month of June, 1782, he with the utmost difficulty made his way through many interruptions of the enemy to the Province of South Carolina, where his Majesty's troops then lay; and that he was obliged to leave the province where he lived, and his property, which we are informed was considerable; and that he is now without the means of subsistence, having lost his all for and on account of his services and attachment to his Majesty's person and government.

JOHN HAMILTON, *Lt.-Col. Com. R.N.C. Regt.*
JOHN LEGETT, *Capt. R.N.C. Regt.*
ALEX. CAMPBELL, *Capt. S.C. Regt.*
GEO. DAWKINS, *Capt. S.C. Regt.*
DANIEL McNEIL,* *Capt. R.N.C. Regt.*
MOSES WHITLEY, *Lieut. S.C. Regt.*
St. Augustine, 20th September, 1783.

On the 25th November following, I drew up an estimate of the loss I had sustained during the late war in America, a true copy of which I hereto set forth:

Schedule of the property of Col. David Fanning, late resident of the Province of North Carolina, but now of the Province of East Florida, lost to him on account of zeal and attachment to the British Government, and never received any part or parcel thereof, or any restoration of same, viz:

550 acres of land in Amelia County in the Province of Virginia, with a dwelling house and other necessary buildings, a large apple and peach orchard, and large enclosed £ s
improvements 687.10

550 acres of land near said plantation, as heir to the estate of my father, and some improvement with a dwelling house . 412.00

3 saddle horses.................................... 41.00

12 plantation do., three unbroke do. 96.00

2 negro slaves..................................... 100.

Debts in notes, bonds, etc......................... 289.

£1,625.10

Personally appeared before me, one of his Majesty's Justices of the Peace, St. Augustine and Province of East Florida, the above-mentioned Col. David Fanning, who, being duly sworn and maketh oath on the Holy Evangelist of Almighty God, that he lost all and every part of the above-mentioned property on account of his zeal and attachment to his Majesty's cause during the late war against the revolted colonies in North America; and that he had not let, sold, bargained, bartered or disposed or impowered any person or persons to let, sell, bargain, barter or dispose of any part or parcel of the same in any manner whatsoever, nor received any restitution for the same. Sworn at St. Augustine, the 25th November, 1783, before me.

JOHN MILLS, J.P.
DAVID FANNING.

Personally appeared before me, one of his Majesty's Justices of the Peace in St. Augustine, Province of East Florida, Lieutenant Charles Robertson, Neill McInnis, and Philip Whisenhunt, refugees, of said East Florida, who being called upon by the within mentioned Col. David Fanning to value the within mentioned property, who being duly sworn, make oath upon the Holy Evangelists of Almighty God, that the within mentioned properties are well worth the sums affixed to each article, as near the value as possible if the same was to be sold, to their own knowledge and the best information they could get.

CHARLES ROBERTSON.
NEIL MCINNIS.
PHILIP WHISENHUNT

Sworn at St. Augustine, this 25th November, 1783, before me.

JOHN MILLS, J.P.

(Here follows notarial certificate by John Mills)

After my many scenes and passages through and during the late war, and often hearing the Americans had got their request, I never could put any faith in it until I saw the King's speech, of which I have hereunto set forth a true copy for the better satisfaction of those loyalists that perhaps have never seen it yet.

New York, February 9th, 1783.

By the brigantine *Peggy*, Capt. McNeil, in nineteen days from Tortola, we have received the following copy of his Majesty's most gracious speech to both houses of Parliament on Thursday, December 5th, 1782—which was brought to Tortola from Windward by Capt. Rodney, son of Lord Rodney:

MY LORDS AND GENTLEMEN:

Since the close of the last session, I have employed my whole time in the care and attention which the important and critical conjuncture of public affairs required of me.

I lost no time in giving the necessary orders to prohibit the further prosecution of offensive war upon the continent of North

America, adopting, as my inclination will always lead me to do with decision and effect, whatever I collect to be the sense of my Parliament and my people. I have pointed all my views and measures as well in Europe as in North America to an entire and cordial reconciliation with those colonies.

Finding it indispensable to the attainment of this object, I did not hesitate to go the full length of the powers vested in me and offered to declare them free and independent States by an article to be inserted in the treaty of peace. Provisional articles are agreed upon to take effect whenever terms of peace shall be finally settled with the court of France. In thus admitting their separation from the crown of these kingdoms, I have sacrificed every consideration of my own to the wishes and opinion of my people. I make it my humour and ever my prayers to Almighty God that Great Britain may not feel the evils which might result from so great a dismemberment of the Empire, and that America may be free from those calamities which have formerly proved in the mother country how essential monarchy is to the enjoyment of constitutional liberty. Religion, language, interest, affections, may and I hope will yet prove a bond of permanent union between the two countries—to this neither attention nor disposition shall be wanting on my part.

While I have carefully abstained from all offensive operations against America, I have directed my whole force by land and sea against the other powers at war with as much vigour as the situation of that force at the commencement of the campaign would permit. I trust that you must have seen with pride and satisfaction the gallant defence of the Governor and garrison of Gibraltar, and my fleet after having effected the object of their destination offering battle to the combined force of France and Spain on their own coasts; those of my kingdom have remained at the same time perfectly secure, and your domestic tranquility uninterrupted. This respectable state under the blessing of God I attribute to the entire confidence which subsists between me and my people, and to the readiness which has been shewn by my subjects in my city of London and in other parts of my kingdoms to stand forth in the general defence. Some proofs have lately been given of public spirit in private men which would do honour to any age and any country—having manifested to the whole world by the most lasting examples the signal spirit and bravery of my people. I conceived it a moment not unbecoming my dignity, and thought it a regard due to the lives and fortunes of such brave and gallant subjects to shew myself ready on my part to embrace fair and honourable terms of accommodation with all the powers at war.

I have the satisfaction to acquaint you that negotiations to this effect are considerably advanced, the result of which as soon as they are brought to a conclusion shall be immediately communicated to you. I have every reason to hope and believe that I shall have it in my power in a very short time to acquaint you that they have ended in terms of pacification which I trust you will see just cause to approve. I rely, however, with perfect confidence on the wisdom of my Parliament and the spirit of my people, that if any unforeseen change in the disposition of the belligerent powers should frustrate my confident expectations, they will approve of the preparations I have thought it advisable to make, and be ready to second the most vigorous efforts in the further prosecution of the war.

GENTLEMEN OF THE HOUSE OF COMMONS:

I have endeavoured by every measure in my power to diminish the burthens of my people. I lost no time taking the most decided measures for introducing a better economy in the expenditure of the army.

I have carried into strict execution the several reductions in my civil list expenses directed by an act of the last session. I have introduced a further reform into other departments and suppressed several sinecure places in them. I have by this means so regulated my establishments that my expense shall not in future exceed my income.

I have ordered the estimate of the civil list debt laid before you last session to be completed. The debt proving somewhat greater than could be then correctly stated and the proposed reduction not immediately taking place, I trust you will provide for deficiency, securing as before the repayment out of my annual income.

I have ordered enquiry to be made into the application of the sum voted in support of the American sufferers, and I trust you will agree with me that a due and generous attention ought to be shown to those who have relinquished their properties or professions from motives of loyalty to me and attachment to the mother country.

* This and the shooting of Capt. Doudy *supra*, appear unjustifiable; but by "bad men" Fanning evidently means men who had murdered Loyalists, and Doudy had broken his parole. Both occurred after Balfour's pronouncement in the negotiation for peace that "there was no resting place for a Tory's foot on the earth."

* This was the grandfather of the recently deceased eminent physician and public man, Hon. Daniel McNeill Parker, M.D., of Nova Scotia.

CHAPTER 6

On the 10th of March I had some business to St. Augustine, the inhabitants of Musqueto asked the favour of me to hand a petition to his Excellency the Governor, and knowing the situation of the petitioners I spoke in their behalf; asked his Excellency what answer he sent to the people, he said he should send for none of them, and if they were a mind to remove, they must get to the shipping as they could, for he said he had no vessels at that time in Government's services.

"To his Excellency Patrick Tonyn, Esq., Capt. General, Governor and Commander and Chief in and over his Majesty's province of East Florida and vice-admiral of the same: whereas your humble petitioners showeth that they are rendered very poor and unable to remove ourselves to be in readiness to receive the opportunity offered for our removement from his Majesty's province of this East Florida which is to be evacuated; here is several poor widows as well as poor men of his Majesty's loyal subjects; we pray his Excellency would send a schooner to remove us to the vessels provided for our passage when his Excellency sees that this province will be given up; we would wish to tarry here where we have good warm houses till his Excellency sees the time draws nigh; however, we would wish to refer it to his Excellency's opinion upon the matter, and in granting of your petitioners' humble petition, your humble petitioners ever will be in duty bound to pray.

At the Musqueto, this 26th of January 1784.
THOMAS YOUNG, Capt. S.C. Mil.
Abraham Floyd, Joseph Currie, Magee Black, Agnes Wilson, Moses Barnes, Jacob Barns, Joseph Rogers."

I left St. Augustine the 13th of said month and returned to the Musqueto and made the following speech to the inhabitants:

My good and worthy friends: I am now going to make some remarks as to your disagreeable situation. The distresses to which the unfortunate loyalists in America are now reduced are too poignant not to command the pity and commiseration of every friend to human nature. The man that is steeled against such a forcible impression is a monster that should be drove from the circle of cultivated society. In most situations, when calamities and misfortunes press upon their minds, hope buoys us up and keeps us from sinking into the ocean of despondency and despair, but the unfortunate loyalists have no hopes to cheer up their spirits; even this last refuge of the afflicted is denied us of enjoying peace and happiness which our forefathers and ourselves were born under. During a seven years' war we have been induced to brave every danger and difficulty in support of the Government under which we were born, in hopes that we and our children would reap the fruits of our labour in peace and serenity. Instead of that reasonable expectation, we find ourselves at the conclusion of a war sacrificed to the indignation of their enemies, expelled their native country, and thrown on the wide world friendless and unsupported. It is needless to repeat the many promises of support and protection held out to the public by the King and those acting under his authority. These promises have been violated in every instance, and that national faith which we had been accustomed to look upon as sacred, basely bartered for an inglorious peace, even to this province for which the loyalists from the other colonies have fled to for shelter are denied us. The Spaniards are in a short time to take possession of this province, and whilst we are together we had better draw up a decent petition to have protection, and throw ourselves on their mercy. If they deny us we will have few to condemn us, which cruel and relenting necessity may compel them to adopt. Innumerable are the difficulties at present to encounter. Stripped of our property, drove from our homes, excluded from the company and care of their dearest connections, robbed of the blessing of a free and mild government, betrayed and deserted by our friends, what is it can repay them for their misery, dragging out a wretched life of obscurity and want? Heaven only that smooths the rugged paths of life can reconcile us to our misfortunes. Also, my hopes of ever receiving anything from Government for losses or services are vanished, as I cannot support any other opinion than whenever Great Britain sees it her interest to withdraw her force and protection from us, let us go where we will, we never can say we are safe from difficulties as we have been induced to brave since the commencement of the late war, and for the same reason I shall in a few days get out in open boats to West Florida to settle myself at or near Fort Notches on the Mississippi River.

On the 20th of March myself and seven other families set out, all in open boats. We kept company for 160 miles. I then left them and went forward to get to better hunting ground, and proceeded until I got to the Scibirsken, where I waited for the rest of my company twelve days; but not seeing them come, I concluded they had passed me, and must have proceeded on their journey. I hoisted sail and stood on until I cam to Key West, and seing a large schooner I stood for her. She hove to, and when I came alongside she informed me that I was then on the edge of the Gulf of Mexico, and then I turned and stood for that key. I got to the key at three o'clock, and the wind blew a gale for fifteen days, and whilst on board the before-mentioned schooner, who belonged to the Spaniards. They had some Creek Indians on board, and then bound to Havana; the Spaniards I could not understand, but they understood the Creek language and my speaking to the Indians and informing of the Indians that I was going to Mississippi, he told me that my boat was too small, and it would be impossible for me to make the main land, as it was three days' sail before I could make land. The Spaniards understood all my discourse, and upon finding where I was bound, they spoke to me in Indian and told me that there were six or seven families of the English had left St. Augustine some time before, and that they were all killed except the negroes, and they thought we would stand a poor chance to escape them, as I should be obliged to keep the shore. In an hour after I made the key there came another Spanish schooner to anchor that I had passed the day before. They could not speak any English, but finding that the others could speak Creek, I also spoke to them in the same language, which they understood very well, and informed me as the other schooner had done. They were windbound for fifteen days, and treated me with every civility. I had one white lad of eighteen years of age, and by the different accounts we had of the Spaniards he got scared. I told him not to lose his life on my account. He then went on board of the schooner, and on the night she wind abated, the Spaniards came on shore and took the most of myself and wife's wearing apparel and bedding.

They informed me before their departure that they looked upon it that we could not proceed with our small open boats, the distance of the bay where we had to cross being about 36 leagues to a key called Sandy Key, which is nine leagues from the main land, which in case of our not hitting that key the distance would be about 100 leagues before we should make land again. Upon which I turned and went back about twelve leagues to Key Bockes, and steered due north till we made the key, being about eight hours out of sight of land. When we made the key, being 19th of said month, I got to said land the 20th. I saw a small schooner standing for the land about four leagues distance from us, and cast anchor where the aforementioned Spaniards informed us that the Indians were very bad in killing the English people that crossed the Bay of Tompay, as the man that started with me being much alarmed at the behaviour of the Indians, set off back again with the Spaniards to the Havana. I then with my little family, consisting of my wife, self and two little negroes, I perceiving it might be dangerous for me to proceed, went on board the little schooner that lay at anchor about four leagues from me. I immediately took my boats and went on board of him, enquiring of one Baptist, who commanded her. I found he was an Italian; asked him where he was from, he informed me from New Providence. I then applied to him to get a passage with him. He told me he could not tell me at that time whether he could carry all my property or not, desired me to pay my boats off that night. The next morning he told me he could not give me a passage for less than 200 dollars. The next day he fell to 150 dollars. Then the wind blowing very fresh, I went on board my boat, and hoisted sail and went off for the land again. In the course of two or three hours he came round a point with a schooner to the land in order to mend some turtle nets which were much broken. He, during the time of his laying there, gave us liberty to come and sleep on board, and on the 23rd of the month I asked him if he would not take less than 150 dollars to carry me to Providence, as I told him I could not afford to give him so much, as it was more than I was able to give him, as I was entirely robbed of what little I had. He said he would not take less. The next morning I set off in my boat and sent my girl along shore to catch some fowls I had on shore, where I was to come back again to the place as soon as I got the distance of about three miles round a point. When I got to the point I left my boat ashore, and went back in order to meet the girl where I expected to see her. I got about half the distance, but did not meet her, and coming there and not finding her I went some little distance back to where the schooner lay. As I expected, they were going to use me in the same manner the Spaniards had done before, when I saw them take my negro girl and carry her on board with them. I then set down for the space of half hour, and considering within myself what I had best do, and seeing the said Baptist, commander of the said schooner, and his man Thomas coming ashore again, after carrying my negro girl off into the woods and hid her. I then saw them coming out of the woods. Thinking within myself that they intended to kill me, with which I looked and examined my gun and powder; finding I had only one charge with me or nigher than my boats, and considering the present distressed situation I was in, obliged me to consider what was my best measure to pursue, and I immediately advanced towards them, they parting, one turned back to where the girl was, the other coming on a small distance, went from the beach and turned off into the woods. I immediately ran and called to him and asked him concerning what he had done with the girl, with which he denied having seen her. I then told him he need not deny it, for I had seen him with her, and offered him four dollars if he would inform me where she was, so that I could get her. He immediately said that Mr. Baptist had the command of the schooner, and that I had better go back and speak to him myself. I also went back to where their boat lay, and continued there for the space of fifteen minutes, then I turned and walked back from the place I started from. During the course of my walking I looked behind and saw the said Baptist about 150 yards in my rear, his gun lying across his left arm. I turned around and advanced to him, and when near him I observed his gun cocked. I asked him at first what he had his gun cocked for; his answer was in order to fire at anything that came. With that I told him that he had better uncock his gun as I did not see anything to fire at there. I told him several times; he replied he always carried his gun cocked, and kept her cocked for the space of fifteen minutes. I asked if he had not seen my girl come that way. He told me no. I then told him that he need not deny it, for I had seen her on board his boat, he being in the boat at the same time, carrying her off to the schooner, not mentioning to him that I saw him bring her back. I then told him I could carry him back and show him the girl's tracks where he had carried her along and took her on board. I then offered him four dollars to give her up, as I told him my present situations would not admit of my giving him as much money as he asked to carry me to Providence. He told me I talked like a boy, as no person would carry me to Providence under five hundred dollars, and he only asked one hundred and fifty, and also alluded to my going off and not speaking to him any more, and that if he had my girl he would keep her as he had lost a boy that cost him eight hundred dollars, and that he must make something before he returned to Providence. I asked him if he would carry me for either the boy or girl, allowing me fifty dollars. He told me no. I told him that it was but little less than the half I was worth; he told me he would carry me for one of them, or fifty dollars. In my distressed situation, and my wife being pregnant, I thought I had best endeavour to get a passage with him. I told him that I would sooner than to lose my negro girl give him one hundred and fifty dollars than either the girl or the boy, as I was convinced I should have justice done me on my arrival at New Providence, as I should see some persons who were acquainted with me in Providence; he told me he would. I then told him I wanted him to drop his schooner down to where my boats were in order to get my property out of the boats. He told me he could not as he was going round the Key to turtle. I then going back, I met with the other man and wanted to hire him. He told me he could not unless I had got liberty from Baptist. With that I went myself, and came to my boats and told my wife the situation of matters, as we immediately started with only my boy's assistance and rowed back against the wind blowing fresh for seven miles; then coming very near the schooner I threw out my anchor and lay there all night, and the next morning I called to them several times and asked them if they had seen my girl. After some time they answered me, Ay, Ay! and told us to come alongside. I told them I wanted my girl to come and assist me in taking out my property. They answered me they would assist me in taking them out. With that I weighed anchor and went alongside of the schooner and told my wife to go on board. When on board she went and called the girl several times. My wife then went down into the hold with a stick, and she said that she found the girl hid among the sails, being stripped of all her clothes she had on the day when she left me. I had my property put on board, and soon after I set off to the shore and anchored my large boat some little distance from the shore, where I lay till some time in June, round the point where I came from, as the wind was blowing fresh. On the 15th of June he got his turtle and water on board where he had his turtle in a crawl in the Bay of Fundy, where he had supplied himself with wood and water, and all his turtle on board, where he then drew a note of hand for me to sign for two hundred pieces of eight for my passage. I immediately answered him I would sooner suffer death than to sign any instrument of writing. He then wished himself damned before I should go with him, and ordered me to haul up my boat and put what I could in her and go on shore with my family. My boat being so small would not carry one-fourth part of my propety off. As there lay a large boat alongside that they had brought off their turtle wood and water on board in, I asked them for the loan of her. They told me they could not as they were going to get under way. With that I brought my boat alongside, and they in the meantime took their two boats and went on shore.

My wife being in a bad situation, fell a crying and begged of me to do anything to get away for fear we might meet with others who might distress us of everything. As I found that I should lose the greatest part in case I went on shore, as I had left my large boat at Cape Sable on the mainland, and my little boat not being large enough to contain over the one-fourth of my property, for which I told him to draw a note for one hundred and fifty dollars, for which I signed, the note being dated 15th July, and was to be paid after my arrival in Providence, to have thirty-five days after my landing there before payment was to be made.

On the 30th of June, as we were laying at New Madamcumba after our having several words, he told me that he understood by my negroes that I intended to have him hung after my arrival at New Providence if he had turned my wife on shore, and in case she had died that I should do my endeavours to hang him in Providence, and told me if it had not been for killing my wife he would be damned if he did not drown me overboard long ago, only on account of my wife. On the 12th July a Capt. Bunch, Capt. Clutsam, and Capt. Wm. Smith, of New Providence, appeared, and Capt. Bunch came on board the small schooner commanded by the said Baptist. The said Mr. Bunch asked me my reasons for staying so long on board that small schooner, and why I gave the said Baptist my note of hand for one hundred and fifty dollars, of which Mr. Bunch informed me that it was contrary to the laws of the Government of New Providence to make any agreement with any person or persons found in distress, but to render every assistance. With this I found Mr. Bunch wished to render me a service in my distressed situation, and I opened to him all former proceedings respecting the ill treatment and behaviour of the said Baptist. On the same account every gentleman of them offered me any assistance I wanted, and Mr. Bunch told me that in case I did not get a passage with Capt. Clutsam, which he did not doubt but what I should, he would give me a passage himself. However, I procured a passage from Capt. Clutsam for fifty dollars, during which passage I was in every respect used and treated like a gentleman by the said Capt. Clutsam, and on my arrival at New Providence the said Capt. Clutsam behaved with so much honour that, instead of taking fifty dollars of me, he deducted twenty, and only charged me thirty, and upon finding who I was would not take but twenty dollars, and he at the same time refused taking any more of me. During the course of my being on board of Capt. Clutsam he found me in every necessary, and made no charge for any provisions or anything I received from him. His humanity was so great, that if ever in my power to render any service to him or any of those gentlemen, nothing shall every be wanting on my part to do them service.

I continued in Nassau for twenty days, and then took my passage with Capt. Jacob Bell to New Brunswick, where we cast anchor 23rd of Sept., 1784, and continued until the 25th of October, and then set out for Halifax to his Excellency Governor Parr, to know how I should get land, but as I got to Halifax his Excellency Governor Carlton arrived, and I could do nothing, so I returned on the 7th November, and in August I received the following letter from Col. John Hamilton in answer to mine in regard to my claims:

DEAR SIR,—I received yours of the 9th February, 1785, a few days ago and notice the contents. I am sorry to inform you that your claims are not yet given in, but I expect the office for receiving claims will be opened again by act of Parliament this session, when you may depend proper care shall be taken of yours. I am sorry to hear of your losses. I hope you are now agreeably settled, and making something for your family. I think if you can leave your business in proper hands, a trip to this country would be of service to you, though I don't think you would get half-pay. Government would settle an annuity on you for life; which cannot be done without your coming here.

If you come you may depend on all my interest in your favour, and I cannot help thinking it worth your while to come home.

I am, dear sir, your humble servant,

JOHN HAMILTON.

London, May 10th, 1785

In a short time after I heard that there was another act of Parliament passed to receive claims for losses and services, also that the Commissioners had arrived at Halifax, and on the 20th March, I set out for Halifax, and presented a copy of my claim from East Florida, with the Memorial as follows:

"To the Honourable Commissioners, appointed by act of Parliament, further to enquire into the losses and services of the American Loyalists.

The Memorial of David Fanning, late Colonel of the North Carolina Militia, humbly sheweth: That your Memorialist is a loyalist from North Carolina, who uniformly and religiously adhered to his duty and loyalty to the best of Sovereigns, for which he suffered persecution, and many other inconveniences—that your Memorialist, by a warrant from Major Craig, of the 82nd Regiment, then commanding at Wilmington, was placed at the head of the militia of that province; that your Memorialist during the late war did command from one to nine hundred and fifty men, with whom he was engaged in six and thirty skirmishes in North Carolina, and four in South Carolina; all of which were of his own planning and in which he had the honour to command; that your Memorialist killed many of the rebels and took many of them prisoners; among the latter of whom were Governor Burke, his council, and many officers of distinction in the rebel army; that your Memorialist, during that time, was twice wounded, and fourteen times taken prisoner; that, on the conclusion of the late peace, your memorialist settled two hundred and fifty souls in East Florida; and himself having taken refuge in several parts of his Majesty's remaining possessions in America, finally settled in the Province of New Brunswick, where he is in great distress, with his family. That your Memorialist, in consequence of his said loyalty to his Sovereign, the many services rendered him, and attachment to the British Government, had his property, real and personal, seized, confiscated, and sold by rebel authority. Your Memorialist therefore prays that his case may be taken into consideration, in order that he may be enabled under your report to receive such aid or relief as his case may be found to deserve."

DAVID FANNING.

St. John, March 1st, 1786.

I also took the following oath before Peter Hunter, Secretary to the Commissioners, in favour of my claim in Halifax:

Town of Halifax, }
  Nova Scotia. } S.S.

David Fanning, late of North Carolina, Colonel of Militia, but now of Kings County, in the Province of New Brunswick, maketh oath and saith that he resided in East Florida and the Bahama Islands from the 15th day of July, 1783, to the 25th of March, 1784, and this deponent further saith that he was utterly incapable of preferring or delivering to the Commissioners appointed by Act of Parliament passed in the twenty-third year of his present Majesty, entitled an Act for appointing Commissioners to enquire into the losses and services of all such persons who have suffered in their rights, properties and possessions, during the late unhappy dissensions in America in consequence of their loyalty to his Majesty and attachment to the British Government, or at this office any Memorial Claim or request for aid or relief on account of this deponent's losses during the late unhappy dissensions in America, within the limited time by the said Act for the receiving of such claims by the reason that this deponent during all such time, viz., Between the 15th July, 1783, and the 25th March, 1784, lived or resided in East Florida and the Bahama Islands; that this deponent did, however, send a claim to Col. John Hamilton, of the North Carolina Volunteers in England, of his losses, but that by a letter that this deponent received from said Hamilton, bearing date 10th May, 1785, he is informed that his claims were not then given to the Commissioners in England, and that this deponent believes his said claim must have arrived in London after the time appointed by the late Act of Parliament for receiving such claims had expired, or that the Colonel, Hutchins, to whom I had entrusted the delivery of the said claim had neglected the trust reposed in him in giving in my claim.

Sworn this _____ day of March, 1786, before me_____

DAVID FANNING.

When I presented my Memorial and estimate of claim to Peter Hunter, Secretary to the Commissioners, he gave me no manner of satisfaction, and on my asking him if I could come under an examination, he told me to be gone, he did not think the Commissioners would receive my claim. When I found I could get no hearing at Halifax at that time, I returned home with a full resolution never to trouble myself any more. At the time of being in Halifax I met my old friend, Capt. John Legett, of the Royal North Carolina Regiment, who said he would speak to the Commissioners in my favour. He also gave me a copy of the following letter from Lieut.-Col. Arch. McKay:

LONDON, Nov. 15th, 1785.

DEAR CAPTAIN,—

Ever mindful of your good-will and the kindness you showed unto me since I had the pleasure of being acquainted with you, induces me to write you a few lines at present informing you of my success since I came to England, knowing you would be glad to hear of the provision made for me. When I came to England, I got a hearing by the Commissioners of American Claims, and they granted me thirty pounds yearly for temporary subsistence. I then laid in a memorial to Sir George Young for Captain's half-pay; but I must confess I thought my chances for that bad enough, as I was not acquainted with any of the Generals who commanded in America; but since it was only amusement to try, I got a certificate from Col. Craig, and another from Col. Hamilton and laid them in with the memorial. It was, with a good many others, a long time from office to office; at length they have allowed me seventy pounds sterling, yearly, for life, for my services in America, exclusive of the other thirty pounds. Upon the whole I do not repent coming to London, as things have turned out.

I wrote to Capt. McNeill this morning, not thinking I should have time to write to you before the ship sailed, and I had not time to write to him so fully as I could wish, but I will mind better next time.

I intend to spend next summer in Scotland, if everything turns out here to my expectations, and I would be glad to get a long letter from you concerning your new settlements. You will please to write to me, under cover to Messrs. John and Hector McKay, No. 5, Crown Court, Westminster; and if I am in Britain I shall be sure to get any letter that may come for me. After my jaunt to Scotland I hope to do myself the honour to call and see you on my way to New Providence, where Alexander and Malcom McKay are gone. I am, sir, with due respect,

Your sincere friend and humble servant,

ARCHIBALD McKAY."

To Capt. John Legett.

I returned home and continued until the 27th June, 1787. When I was entering the suburbs of the city of St. John, I accidentally met Ensign Henry Niss, with a letter from the Commissioners, desiring me to attend immediately for an examination. I still retained my opinion, but on informing Col. Joseph Robinson, he prevailed with me, after a long persuasion, to call and see the Commissioners, which I did, in company with Col. Robinson, where I was treated with every civility and all attention paid to me. After my examination they gave me the following certificate:

"OFFICE OF AMERICAN CLAIMS,

St. John, 2nd February, 1787.

We do hereby certify that David Fanning has undergone an examination on oath before us, as an American sufferer from North Carolina. We are satisfied by his own account, and by the evidence he has produced, that his exertions in support of the British Government, as Colonel of the Chatham and Randolph County Militia, during the late troubles in America, have been very great and exemplary; that he has been severely wounded in several engagements and has in other respects been a great sufferer; though, from particular reasons, it will not be in our power to make him any considerable allowance under our report. We therefore recommend him as a proper person to be put on the half-pay list as Captain, and to have an annual allowance from Government equal to that half-pay.

THOMAS DUNDAS.

J. PEMBERTON."

I then empowered George Randall, Esq., Whitehall, London, to act for me. I sent the original certificates and memorial in company with the letter.

To the Right Honourable Sir George Younge, Baronet, Secretary at War, etc., etc.:

The Memorial of David Fanning, late Colonel of the Chatham and Randolph County Militia, in North Carolina, humbly sheweth:

That in the year 1781, under an appointment from Major Henry Craig, then commanding the British troops in North Carolina, your Memorialist embodied near one thousand men of the loyal inhabitants of that Province, and with them performed singular service to the British Government; that he has been twice severely wounded in the course of the war; he has been fourteen times taken prisoner, and has been tried for his life by the rebels, and has ever exerted his utmost endeavours in support of the cause of Great Britain; he is disabled by wounds he has received and has no means of support. For the truth of these allegations he begs to refer to his appointment of Colonel, to the certificates of several officers under whom he served, and to the certificates of the Commissioners of American Claims, forwarded herewith.

Your Memorialist most humbly prays that he may be put on the Provincial half-pay list as Captain, fully confident that his past

78

services and present necessitous situation will be thought deserving of that appointment, and your Memorialist, as in duty bound, shall every pray,

DAVID FANNING.

City of St. John, 2nd February, 1787.

Pursuant to the advice of Lieut.-Col. Joseph Robinson, I have transmitted a power of attorney to you in order to receive half-pay, with a certificate from the Commissioners. Mr. I. Pemberton and Colonel Dundas, Esq.; General Alexander Leslie, Col. Nisbet Balfour, Lieut.-Col. J. Henry Craig, of the 16th Regiment, and Lieut.-Col. John Hamilton, of the North Carolina Regiment, are witnesses of my services. If you will be so good as to accept the power and grant me your assistance in obtaining the same, you will highly oblige,

Sir, your most obedient humble servant,

DAVID FANNING.

New Brunswick,
 City of St. John, February 7th, 1787.
GEORGE RANDALL, ESQ., WESTMINSTER,
 WHITEHALL, LONDON.

Received July 20th, 1787, the following from my agent:

WHITEHALL, 15th May, 1787.

SIR,—On the 3rd inst., in a letter to Lieut.-Col. Robinson, I desired he would inform you of my having received your Memorial, Certificate, etc., claiming the half-pay of a Captain or a military pension equal to the rank. Since than I have received your letter with duplicates of the above papers, and your bill of £260 1s. has been presented as you desired, and as I was also much disposed to do. I have the holder a favourable answer and the true one, that you had reason to expect that I should have effects in hand sufficient to pay the bill when it became due, but that a delay in settling your business, and which you could not foresee, would for a time prevent my accepting your bill.

I must now inform you that I took the earliest opportunity of presenting your memorial and the certificate of the Commissioners, being highly honourable to you and recommending you for an allowance, or the half-pay of Captain. I think there is no reason to doubt you will have a sum equal to that rank allowed you by Government. You had omitted to request that the grant might take place from the 24th of October, 1783, but I added a paragraph to the memorial for that purpose, but whether you will be allowed

79

from that period is doubtful. I am sorry at the same time to acquaint you that it may be some months before the determination of Government is known, but you may be sure tht I shall pay a particular attention to your business and give you the earliest notice of the event. The certificate you sent, though very regular as to the periods, I think would not entitle me to receive the money from the pay office on your account, as I am inclined to believe your allowance will be a military allowance, and not half-pay, and for that reason I send you a printed certificate, which you can keep as a precedent, and desire you will transmit to me a sett, copied from it, for the same periods as them you have already transmitted, taking particular care that there be no blot, alteration or erasure in the dates. I will be much obliged to you if you will acquaint Chillas that the answer of Government to his memorial is that he cannot be placed on the half-pay establishment, the commission he held being only in the militia of the town of New York.

The packet you sent with the certificate amounted to 12 shillings postage and your single letter to one shilling.

I am, sir, your most obedient humble servant,

GEORGE RANDALL.

To David Fanning.

WHITEHALL, 1st August, 1787.
SIR,—On the 15th May, I acknowledged the receipt of your letter and duplicate containing memorials, certificates and other papers relating to your claim of half-pay, or a military pension, and acquainted you that having presented those papers, I thought you had a very fair prospect of success. I am still of that opinion, but am sorry to acquaint you that the consideration of half-pay claims is again deferred and that it may be some months longer before I can acquaint you with the results. I conclude, therefore, that the bill you drew on me for £260 1s. must be returned.

I have received from the Treasury the sum granted to you by Government on account of your losses, for which I gave a receipt in the annexed form and am ready to accept your bill for £22 14s., as after deducting agency and postage, etc., and abstract herewith sent.

Copy of a receipt:

The 24th day of July, 1787, received of Mr. Thomas Coffin by order of the Lords of the Treasury and according to a distribution under the direction of the Commissioners of American Claims, appointed by an Act of the 23rd of his present Majesty, the sum of

£24, as a payment for present relief and on account of the losses during the late dissensions in America.
Signed for David Fanning,

G. RANDALL, *Attorney*

£24 0S.

After this I received the letter from my Agent and found I had lost property to the amount of £1,625 10S. according to an appraisement of three men acquainted with the property. But, as it was not like a coat taken out of my hand, or gold taken out of my pocket, I could not get anything for my losses, although I did not give in anything like the amount of my losses. I lost twenty-four horses, and only reported fifteen, one of which cost more than all I ever got from Government, and six head of cattle, £289 for property sold at the commencement of the war, and the land which I was heir to, and for which I refused, many times, £3,000 Virginia currency. But because I turned out in the service of my King and country in the 20th year of my age, and my exertions were very exemplary in support of the British Government, I have lost my all, for and on account of my attachment to the British Government—only £60, which would not pay the expenses I have been at to obtain it.

I can prove what I have here wrote to be facts, and the world will be able to judge after reading this narrative, and observe this Act of Oblivion passed in North Carolina, in the year 1783, which is herewith set forth—which is enlarged and improved in the *London Magazine*, which will be found on page 607, Vol. I, from July 1 to Dec. 1, 1783.

An Act of Pardon and Oblivion, by the State of North Carolina.

Whereas, it is the policy of all wise States, on the termination of all Civil Wars, to grant an Act of Pardon and Oblivion for past offences, and as divers of the citizens of this State and others, the inhabitants thereof in the course of the late unhappy war, have become liable to great pains and penalties for offences committed against the peace and government of this State, and the General Assembly, out of an earnest desire to observe the articles of peace on all occasions, disposed to forgive offences rather than punish where the necessity for an exemplary punishment has ceased. Be it therefore enacted by the General Assembly of the State of North Carolina, and it is hereby enacted by the authority of the same, that all and all manner of treasons, misprisions of teason, felony or misdemeanour, committed or done since the 4th day of July,

1776, by any persons whatsoever, be pardoned, released and put in total oblivion.

Provided always that this Act or anything herein contained, shall not extend to pardon or discharge, or give any benefit whatsoever to persons who have taken commission or have been denominated officers, and acted as such to the King of Great Britain, or to such as are named in any of the laws commonly called confiscation laws, or to such as have attached themselves to the British and continued without the limits of the State and not returned within twelve months previous to the passing of this Act.

Provided further, that nothing herein contained shall extend to pardon Peter Mallet, David Fanning and Samuel Andrews, or any person or persons guilty of deliberate and wilful murder, robbery, rape or house-breaking, or any of them, anything herein contained to the contrary notwithstanding. Provided, nevertheless, that nothing in this Act shall be construed to bar any citizen of this State from their civil action for the recovery of debts or damage. Provided, also, that nothing herein contained shall entitle any person by this law to be relieved to elect or be elected to any office or trust in this State, or to hold any office civil or military.

And whereas by an Act passed at Wake Court House, all officers, civil and military, who have taken parole were suspended from the execution of their respective offices, and required to appear at the next General Assembly, to shew cause, if any they could, why they should not be removed from the said office; and, whereas, several of the officers aforesaid have neglected to appear agreeably to the requisition of the Act of Assembly. Be it enacted by the General Assembly of the State of North Carolina, and it is hereby enacted, by the authority of the same, that all such officers, both civil and military, are hereby declared to stand suspended from the execution of their several offices until they shall appear at some future Assembly and be restored to the execution of their respective offices or removed agreeable to their merits or demerits. Provided that nothing herein contained shall be construed to exclude a Justice of the Peace from executing the duties of his office, who shall make it appear to the satisfaction of the Court of his County by oath or otherwise; that he was taken prisoner without his consent and privily, and that after his capture he had not voluntarily stayed with the enemy, nor taken an active part in any manner by furnishing them willingly with provisions, bearing arms, or accepting any appointment in their civil regulations.

Read three times and ratified in General Assembly, the 17th May, 1783.

RIC. CASWELL, *S. Senate.*

E. STARKEY, *S. Commons.*

Many people are fools enough to think, because our three names are particularly put in this Act, that we are all guilty of the crimes set forth, but I defy the world to charge me with rape, or anything more than I have set forth in this Journal.

All his Majesty's subjects or others that wish to know the truth of anything further than I have set forth, let them make enquiry of those gentlemen whose names I have struck in; examine the letters of the rebels, and the recommendations of the officers who have been acquainted with me in person and with my services in the time of the late war.

Although I have been prohibited from receiving any benefit from the laws of the State, all that I desire is to have the liberty of commanding 30,000 men in favour of the British Government. I flatter myself that there would be no doubt of my putting many of them to swing by the neck for their honesty, as John White did, after stealing 150 horses in North Carolina.

Here follows a short address to the printer, signed, sir,

Your most obedient and humble servant,

DAVID FANNING.

(*The end*)

www.ingramcontent.com/pod-product-compliance
Lightning Source LLC
Chambersburg PA
CBHW020514030426
42337CB00011B/389